USING A COMPETENCY DEVELOPMENT PROCESS
MODEL IN HIGHER EDUCATION

USING A COMPETENCY DEVELOPMENT PROCESS MODEL IN HIGHER EDUCATION
A Practical Guide

Nancy I. Latham, Johnna Darragh Ernst, Tiffany Freeze, Stephanie Bernoteit, and Bradford R. White

Foreword by Charla S. Long

NEW YORK AND LONDON

First published in 2023 by Stylus Publishing, LLC.

Published in 2023 by Routledge
605 Third Avenue, New York, NY 10017
4 Park Square, Milton Park, Abingdon, Oxon OX14 4RN

Routledge is an imprint of the Taylor & Francis Group, an informa business.

© 2023 Taylor & Francis Group

All rights reserved. No part of this book may be reprinted or reproduced or utilised in any form or by any electronic, mechanical, or other means, now known or hereafter invented, including photocopying and recording, or in any information storage or retrieval system, without permission in writing from the publishers.

Trademark Notice: Product or corporate names may be trademarks or registered trademarks, and are used only for identification and explanation without intent to infringe.

Library of Congress Cataloging-in-Publication-Data

Names: Latham, Nancy, author.
Title: Using a competency development process model in higher education : a practical guide / Nancy I. Latham, Johnna Darragh Ernst, Tiffany Freeze, Stephanie Bernoteit, Bradford R. White ; foreword by Charla S. Long.
Description: First edition. | Sterling : Stylus, 2023. | Includes bibliographical references and index.
Identifiers: LCCN 2023001603
ISBN 9781642670523 (cloth) | ISBN 9781642670530 (paperback)
Subjects: LCSH: Competency-based education--United States. |
Education,
    Higher--United States--Evaluation. | College graduates--Employment--United
    States. | School-to-work transition--United States.
Classification: LCC LC1032 .L37 2023
    DDC 378/.01--dc23/eng/20230208
LC record available at https://lccn.loc.gov/2023001603

ISBN: 9781642670523 (hbk)
ISBN: 9781642670530 (pbk)
ISBN: 9781003448532 (ebk)

DOI: 10.4324/9781003448532

CONTENTS

	LIST OF FIGURES AND TABLES	vii
	FOREWORD *Charla S. Long*	xi
	ACKNOWLEDGMENTS	xiii
	INTRODUCTION	1
1	DEFINE THE PATHWAY PROBLEM	26
2	ESTABLISH THE COMPETENCY FRAMEWORK Analysis of Professional Expectations That Define the Field	42
3	DRAFT COMPETENCY STATEMENTS	56
4	ESTABLISH COMPETENCY MEASURABILITY	69
5	DEVELOP COMPETENCY ASSESSMENTS	87
6	ADOPT AND IMPLEMENT COMPETENCIES IN LEARNING JOURNEY AND CREDENTIALING SYSTEMS	105
7	EVALUATING THE IMPACT OF COMPETENCIES OVER TIME AND SUPPORTING COMPETENCY SUSTAINABILITY	121
	CONCLUSION	131
	ABOUT THE AUTHORS	133
	INDEX	137

LIST OF FIGURES AND TABLES

Introduction

- Figure I.1. Relationship between CBL and CBE.
- Figure I.2. Competency-based education framework continuum.
- Figure I.3. Illinois ECE and Tennessee LTSS competency lexicon.
- Figure I.4. Steps in career pathway progress.
- Figure I.5. A simple representation of the concept of competency.
- Figure I.6. Graphic representation of a competency.
- Figure I.7. The backward design process.

Step 1: Define the Pathway Problem

- Table 1.1 Early Childhood Education Role by Educational Requirements: Teaching Assistant
- Table 1.2 Career Pathway Challenges in Educational and Workplace Contexts

Step 2: Establish the Competency Framework: Analysis of Professional Expectations that Define the Field

- Figure 2.1. Framework origin for the QuILTSS Institute's CBE Certificate in Long-Term Services and Supports (LTSS) program.
- Figure 2.2. CMS Direct Service Workforce Core Competency: Communication.
- Table 2.1 Relationships Between Gateways ECE Benchmarks, Illinois Professional Teaching Standards, and NAEYC Standards for Professional Preparation
- Table 2.2 Course Bundles

Step 3: Draft Competency Statements

- Table 3.1 Gateways ECE Human Growth and Development Assessment
- Table 3.2 LTSS Levels of Mastery—Person-Centered Practices

- Table 3.3 Competency Area Table
- Table 3.4 Stakeholders

Step 4: Establish Competency Measurability

- Figure 4.1. Excerpt example of assessor notes on behavior.
- Figure 4.2. Excerpt example rating scale across discrete behaviors.
- Figure 4.3. Excerpt example of scoring tool with predetermined criteria.
- Table 4.1 ECE Interactions, Relationships, and Environments (IRE1) Binary Scoring Tool
- Table 4.2 ECE Interactions, Relationships, and Environments Leveled Scoring Tool
- Table 4.3 Analyze Performance Indicator Verbs
- Table 4.4 Developing Lower Level Verb Performance Criteria
- Table 4.5 Developing Higher Level Verb Performance Criterion
- Table 4.6 Developing Higher Level Verb Performance Criterion Binary Scoring Tool
- Table 4.7 Leveled Scoring Tool Template
- Table 4.8 Plan for Scoring Tool Reflection and Feedback

Step 5: Develop Competency Assessments

- Figure 5.1. Excerpt example of assessment outline for cultural competency.
- Figure 5.2. Excerpt example of standardized delivery template.
- Table 5.1 Gateways Competencies Assessed
- Table 5.2 HSW Level 1 Assessment Experience
- Table 5.3 HSW Level 3 Assessment Task
- Table 5.4 HSW Level 4 Assessment Task
- Table 5.5 HSW Level 5 Assessment Task
- Table 5.6 ECE Health, Safety, and Wellness Level 2 Assessment Checklist
- Table 5.7 ECE Health, Safety, and Wellness Level 2 Scoring Tool
- Table 5.8 Overview of Assessment Tasks Reflective of Performance Indicators

Step 6: Adopt and Implement Competencies in Learning Journey and Credentialing Systems

- Figure 6.1. Cue card for communication competency.
- Figure 6.2. Registry system.

- Figure 6.3. Employment support pathway.
- Table 6.1 Adopting and Implementing Competencies in Your Credentialing System

Step 7: Evaluating the Impact of Competencies Over Time and Supporting Competency Sustainability

- Figure 7.1. QuILTSS quality framework.
- Table 7.1 Health, Safety, and Well-Being Competency Area Cumulative Evaluation Data Table
- Table 7.2 Goal/Outcome of Competencies on Workforce Challenges

For full versions of Figures I.3, 6.1, and 6.2, visit the link to the Routledge website or scan the QR code.

https://www.routledge.com/Using-a-Competency-Development-Process-Model-in-Higher-Education-A-Practical/Latham-Ernst-Freeze-Bernoteit-White/p/book/9781642670530

FOREWORD

This is a pivotal moment in postsecondary education. Competency-based education (CBE) can enable a much broader array of learners to access education, especially women and people of color. Competency-based education focuses on what a person actually knows and can do, rather on where or how they learned it. By allowing all learning to count and enabling people to get credit for the knowledge, skills, and behaviors they already have, institutions can focus on the competencies learners still need to develop for their chosen field of study. Not only does this allow for differentiated learning pathways based on each individual's needs, this makes credentials more flexible, relevant, and valuable while boosting completion rates and allowing learners to access better careers and advance economically.

With the release of this book, readers can examine two of the more innovative and effective competency-based models in the United States and see firsthand how these accomplished educators built their successful programs. Both programs featured in this book are based on multiyear, statewide efforts to develop competency-based credentials aligned to career and college pathways. Although the disciplines at the core of this work are early childhood education and long-term healthcare, the development approach and the lessons learned can be applied to any field.

For years, I have had the pleasure of walking alongside these authors as they determined their competencies, set performance expectations, wrote authentic assessments, curated dynamic learning journeys, and enrolled learners. The authors have experienced the challenges and rewards that come from building a quality CBE program and they share their experiences—the good and bad—with you, the reader. I am certain this book will save you more than a few headaches along the way.

Learners need a better and more equitable path forward. As educators, I urge you to read this book, put its key lessons into practice, and help the more than 39 million Americans with some college but no degree or credential.

Happy Reading,
Charla S. Long
President
Competency-Based Education Network

ACKNOWLEDGMENTS

Many people contributed to the publication of this book. First, we would like to thank our editor David Brightman of Stylus Publishing for his support and expertise throughout the development of this book. We would also like to thank Agate for their support during the editing process and Will Mason and Emily Chase for their expertise in graphic design.

Special thanks are extended to Joni Scritchlow. Joni not only provided statewide leadership in the development of competencies through her leadership role at the Illinois Network of Child Care Resource and Referral Agencies (INCCRRA), but also lent critical and needed expertise in the editing phases of the manuscript.

Each of our organizations were instrumental in the support and development of this book, including the University of Illinois at Urbana-Champaign, Heartland Community College, the QuILTSS Institute, and the Competency-Based Education Network. We extend thanks to the extensive contributions of early childhood higher education faculty in Illinois and the leadership of INCCRRA, the Illinois Board of Higher Education, the Illinois Governor's Office of Early Childhood Development, the Illinois Department of Human Services, the Illinois Community College Board, the McCormick Foundation, and the Illinois State Board of Education in moving competencies from an idea to a statewide reality. Appreciation is equally extended to the Tennessee long-term services and supports workforce and key stakeholders, the Bureau of TennCare, the Centers for Medicare & Medicaid Services, and The QuILTSS Institute, who developed a competency-based system to ensure that this workforce has the knowledge, skills, and intellectual behaviors needed to perform their critically important work.

INTRODUCTION

What if education aligned with employers to produce learners who are workforce ready? What if education was centered around learning expectations that are held constant regardless of the time it takes a learner to get there? What if education was centered around an experience that supports learner success through elements such as flexible offerings; program alignment across general education and technical area of focus; or opportunities to earn credit for external learning experiences? What if educational programs designed curricula with the end in mind, teaching and assessing only the knowledge and skills necessary for success in the workplace and broader life applications?

Competency-based education (CBE) has become a proposed solution to questions such as these that higher education key stakeholders—namely employers, learners, parents, and even educators themselves—are asking. The literature (Haynes et al., 2016; Irvine & Kevan, 2016; Parsons et al., 2016) suggests several potential advantages that CBE presents over traditional educational models. In the following section, we discuss four primary rationales for CBE—pedagogical motivations, quality assurance, the ability to meet the demands of today's students (adult learners in particular), and the ability to meet the needs of the modern workplace—and explore these themes in more detail.

Pedagogical Motivations

Proponents of CBE argue that this model is better able to provide individualized instructional supports than traditional learning models. For example, several authors note that student-centered features of CBE—including individualized supports and greater autonomy, flexibility, and responsibility over their own learning—are associated with increased academic engagement, motivation, self-efficacy, and other learning capacities that predict academic success (Camacho & Legare, 2016; Haynes et al., 2016). Some of these progressive pedagogical features are borrowed from the "open classroom" movement of the late 1960s and early 1970s. Advocates of this movement suggested that teacher-led classrooms be replaced with a curriculum guided by students' interests that allowed students to learn at their own pace (Le et al., 2014). CBE also borrows from Bloom's "mastery learning" pedagogy, which was popularized in the late 1970s and early 1980s and emphasized assessment as well as varied the time needed to meet learning goals. Additionally, CBE is reflective of Keller's "Personalized System of Instruction," which allowed mastery learning to be more individually paced (Le et al., 2014). CBE is also sometimes associated with the standards movement, which began in the 1980s and introduced common educational objectives with related assessments for all students across a given grade statewide. According to Le et al. (2014), CBE may be viewed as the marriage of the standards movement and the personalization movement, in which students' learning experiences are tailored to their individual needs, skills, and interests. Le et al. note that standards and personalization have often been in opposition, but they can be reconciled by acknowledging the importance of clearly defined learning goals for all while offering individualized strategies for meeting those goals. Further, Le et al. argue that recent advances in the cognitive sciences, motivation theory, social learning, and balanced assessment have important implications for personalized CBE and provide further motivation for pursuing the CBE model. Scholars (Burnette, 2016; Irvine & Kevan, 2016; Le et al., 2014; McCombs & Vakili, 2005) have also observed that modern technology, such as adaptive learning and advances in online instruction, now make it more feasible to pursue CBE on an even larger scale and with greater individualization.

Quality Assurance

A second motivation for CBE is dissatisfaction with the outcomes of traditional postsecondary programs. Employers in the United States have often voiced concerns that college graduates lack valuable knowledge or critical thinking skills, and that training recent graduates is expensive (Laitinen, 2012; Long, 2017). The public, parents of graduates, and graduates themselves have reported similar shortcomings and often view higher education as high in cost and low in productivity (Irvine & Kevan, 2016). For these reasons, many scholars see CBE as a potential avenue for providing some degree of quality assurance for graduates, ensuring that they acquire the knowledge and skills needed for success after college (Klein-Collins, 2013). Long (2017) contrasts the CBE model—working until students understand the content—with the "teach and hope" approach of traditional postsecondary programs—participating until course time runs out. Similarly,

Ganzglass et al. (2011) contend that credit awarded based on competence rather than seat time ensures postsecondary credentials will be accepted and recognized across programs and industries.

Proponents of this approach observe that CBE will improve the *transparency, accountability, portability,* and *comparability* of postsecondary credentials by making it easier to identify the competencies associated with a degree and providing clear documentation that these competencies have been met (Book, 2014; Burnette, 2016; Ganzglass et al., 2011). Proponents of CBE also argue that transparency, accountability, portability, and comparability can increase equity by making career pathways more explicit, thus increasing access and economic mobility for traditionally underserved populations such as racial/ethnic minority students and first-generation college-goers (Lumina Foundation for Education, 2015).

Meeting the Demands of Today's Students (Especially Adult Learners)

Nontraditional students—including those older than 25, those enrolled part time or working full time, and single parents—make up increasingly larger proportions of those pursuing higher education. According to 2008 National Center for Educational Statistics (NCES) data, only 14% of all undergraduates attended college full time and lived on campus (Laitinen, 2012). As of 2015, 40% of undergraduate students were adult learners (age 25 and older), 27% worked full time, and 25% had children (Center for Law and Social Policy, 2015; McClarty & Gaertner, 2015). Although CBE is not limited to adult learners who are already participating in the workforce, such nontraditional students have often been one of the main target audiences and have historically constituted the majority of the student population in CBE programs (Book, 2014; Education Commission of the States, 2017; Parsons et al., 2016). In fact, recent surveys of postsecondary institutions reveal that providing educational options for nontraditional students is one of the most commonly cited motivations for developing CBE programs (Garrett & Lurie, 2016; Lurie et al., 2019). Further, research (Daugherty et al., 2015) suggests that students with work experience and some prior college education are more likely to be successful in CBE programs than more traditional students without prior full-time work experience or prior college education.

The increased enrollment of adult learners looking to "up-skill" has created multiple challenges for the institutions of higher education working to serve them. Such students often need increased flexibility in their course scheduling (in terms of time, location, and course load) and tend to have more limited budgets (Camacho & Legare, 2016; Education Commission of the States, 2017; Ohio Department of Higher Education, 2016). Proponents argue that CBE is well suited to meet the needs of today's students because it is more flexible, efficient, and affordable than traditional higher education programs. According to Mallett (2016), CBE "has the potential to evolve and shape the postsecondary education industry" by shifting from an expensive and highly complicated system to a model that is more affordable, simple, convenient, and accessible (p. 110).

Flexibility

As Long (2017) notes, today's students demand flexible schedules that allow them to accelerate (or decelerate) the pace of credit accumulation to meet their evolving needs. Thus, institutions of higher education need to be adaptable if they hope to attract and successfully serve today's students. Numerous scholars (Fain, 2014; Kelchen, 2015; Porter, 2016) have cited the flexibility of CBE programs as a prime factor in the growth of this model. Further, CBE programs that award credit for work experience or other demonstrations of content mastery can significantly shorten time to degree (Camacho & Legare, 2016; Klein-Collins, 2013; Walters, 2016). This is especially important due to the high prevalence of credit-worthy occupational training in today's workforce—training that is often provided by college faculty or instructors but is typically disassociated from the credit-bearing system (Ganzglass et al., 2011). According to Ganzglass et al., noncredit occupational education makes up nearly half of all postsecondary education, and, in many cases, is academically equivalent to college instruction.

Affordability

Another way CBE responds to the demands of today's students is affordability. Amid growing national concerns about student debt and the increased costs of higher education, CBE is viewed by many as a potential means to improve the efficiency of the higher education system and lower costs to both the student and the institution (Burnette, 2016; Daugherty et al., 2015; Dodge et al., 2018; Irvine & Kevan, 2016; Kelchen, 2015; Lacey & Murray, 2015).

Indeed, the potential for CBE programs to reduce student debt was a prime motivation in President Obama's and Secretary Duncan's advocacy for the model, and some view CBE as the key for breaking the "iron triangle" of tight relationships between cost, access, and quality in higher education (Camacho & Legare, 2016; Long, 2017; Porto, 2013; White House Office of the Press Secretary, 2013). Because CBE is focused on mastery rather than learning time, these programs may reduce the amount of coursework needed for a degree and, in theory at least, decrease the costs of earning a credential (Ohio Department of Higher Education, 2016). However, there has been little research to test whether this theory plays out in reality and allows students to earn degrees and credentials at a lower price when compared to traditional higher education programs (Kelchen, 2015). Some studies have found that credit accumulation in CBE programs varies widely based on the degree to which students can accelerate their coursework or increase their course load—which, in turn, varies widely between programs (Parsons et al., 2016). Although it is *possible* for students to save money by completing a CBE program as opposed to a traditional program, it is also possible for CBE programs to be more expensive, and more research is needed to determine whether savings occur more often with CBE programs. As a result, researchers cannot yet conclude that CBE programs are, on average, more affordable for students. Additional research is also needed to determine whether CBE programs are less (or more) expensive than traditional programs for colleges and universities to administer (Burnette, 2016).

Preparing Graduates for the Modern Workforce

Highly skilled and credentialed employees are in high demand both for the modern workforce and to improve the international standing of the U.S. economy (Burnette, 2016; Le et al., 2014). With the nation losing its global lead in college completion rates and many states committing to the Lumina Foundation's goal of increasing the proportion of the population with high-quality degrees, certificates, and other credentials to 60% by 2025, employers and policymakers are keenly focused on finding innovative ways for more students to access and complete postsecondary education (Education Commission of the States, 2017; Long, 2017; Lumina Foundation for Education, 2015; Parsons et al., 2016). Proponents view CBE as one potential solution to this challenge, due to its ability to provide new pathways for college access and completion (Book, 2014; Daugherty et al., 2015). For instance, the "Connecting Credentials" project, a partnership between the Lumina Foundation and the Corporation for a Skilled Workforce, created a framework for linking credentials with the workforce explicitly through competencies (Connecting Credentials, 2017). In the 2018 National Survey of Postsecondary Competency-Based Education (NSPCBE), improving workforce preparedness was the most commonly cited motivation for institutions that had already begun pursuing CBE (Lurie et al., 2019).

College access and completion are also increasingly important from the individual standpoint. More and more jobs in the modern workforce require postsecondary education and credentials, and education beyond high school has become an economic imperative to achieving employment and success in the workforce (Burnette, 2016; Camacho & Legare, 2016). As noted by Le et al. (2014), "The recognition that most jobs soon will require postsecondary credentials has raised the stakes; graduating from high school is no guarantee of finding any job, let alone a job that pays enough to support a family or leads to a career that does" (p. 6). Further, CBE programs have the potential to be more closely aligned with industry skills and more responsive to employers' needs, thus creating better employment and career outcomes for students (Camacho & Legare, 2016; Daugherty et al., 2015; Ganzglass et al., 2011).

What Is Competency-Based Education and Competency-Based Learning?

Key questions often asked by those considering competency-based programs are: "What is competency-based education?" and "How does CBE compare to other efforts over the years such as competency-based learning (CBL), competency-based assessment, or performance-based education?" *CBE* is defined by the Competency-Based Education Network (C-BEN) in the following way:

> Competency-based education combines an intentional and transparent approach to curricular design with an academic model in which the time it takes to demonstrate competencies varies and the expectations about learning are held constant. Students acquire and demonstrate their knowledge and skills by engaging in learning exercises, activities, and experiences that align with clearly defined programmatic outcomes. Students receive proactive guidance and support from faculty and staff. Learners earn credentials by demonstrating mastery through multiple forms of assessment, often at a personalized pace. (C-BEN, 2021, p. 4)

It is also important here to offer an explanation for CBL and its relationship to CBE. According to C-BEN, CBE is considered a distinct form of CBL. CBL includes formal, informal, and nonformal learning (or learning assessment) opportunities—both self-created and those designed by employers, educational institutions, and training providers—that are aligned to workplace-relevant competencies. Examples of CBL include courses or modules offered by institutions of higher education; prior learning assessment; military credit; other work-based learning; apprenticeships and returnships; industry certifications; and government licensures. In comparison, CBE includes formal learning opportunities that are designed by institutions and lead to recognized educational credentials. CBE is created by backward design from a disciplinary perspective on what a credential-holder should know and be able to do, with a demonstration of mastery required through performance on authentic assessments. Examples of CBE include direct assessment programs and nondirect assessment programs. See Figure I.1 for an illustration of the relationship between CBL and CBE. Programs often use CBL as a vehicle for moving toward preparedness for a full CBE program, while others may use CBL to improve outcomes that make their program more appealing to learners, employers, and other stakeholders. A distinguishing characteristic is that CBE can be viewed from a programmatic approach. A CBE program involves the whole credential; whether a microcredential or full associate degree, for example, the entire credential is thought of as the requirement of full mastery.

It should be highlighted that both direct and nondirect assessment programs are included as CBE. Direct assessment programs allow students to progress at their own pace by demonstrating mastery of competencies on summative assessments. Such programs are not based on traditional academic terms or credit hours (although they may establish "credit-hour equivalencies" for the student learning outcomes they evaluate) but instead award credit and degrees or credentials solely on the basis of mastering competencies (Council of Regional Accrediting Commissions, 2015;

Figure I.1. Relationship between CBL and CBE.

Competency-Based Learning
- Coursed or modules offered by IHEs
- Prior Learning Assessment
- Military credit
- Other work-based learning
- Apprenticeships and returnships
- Industry certifications
- Government licensures

Competency-Based Education
- Direct assessment programs
- Nondirect assessment CBE programs

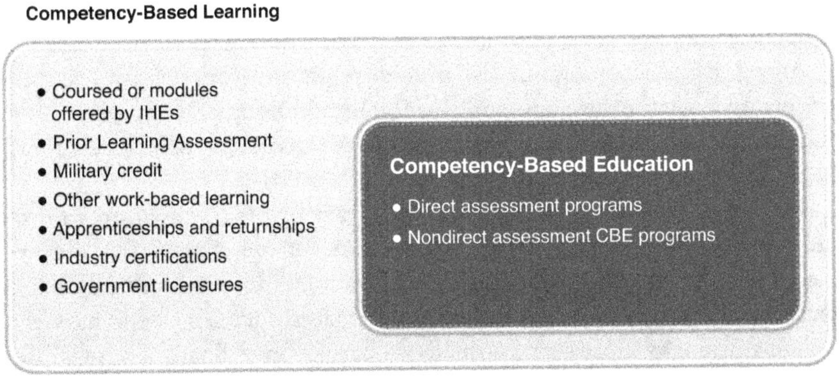

From *A Leader's Guide to Competency-Based Education: From Inception to Implementation* by L. Dodge, D. J. Bushway, & C. S. Long, 2018, Stylus.

Kelchen, 2015). Advanced Placement and International Baccalaureate programs that allow high schoolers to earn college credit are two common examples of direct assessment programs. Often, students in direct assessment programs may be able to receive credit based on work experiences or other out-of-school opportunities for developing knowledge and skills (Camacho & Legare, 2016). According to Kelchen (2015), only 34 institutions offered credit via direct assessment as of 2015. As a result of the 2019 negotiated rulemaking process, direct assessment programs can access Title IV funds with the U.S. Department of Education's approval. Such approval is required for an institution's first direct assessment offering. Nondirect assessment programs include course-based and hybrid programs. In course-based programs, competencies are embedded in conventional coursework linked with credit hours toward a degree or credential (Burnette, 2016; Council of Regional Accrediting Commissions, 2015). This is by far the most common CBE model, with hundreds of colleges currently offering or planning to offer course-based CBE (Fain, 2014). The Tennessee case study of long-term services and supports described in this book is one example of such a course-based CBE approach. Hybrid programs are a blend of course-based and direct assessment models and will be recognized in statute as of effective July 2021 if the program is already established as an approved direct assessment program. The hybrid model allows students to earn degrees or credentials through a combination of direct assessment of competencies and credit hours. The Illinois case study of early childhood education described in this book is one example of such a hybrid CBE approach.

There is considerable room for variation within each of the main CBE models, and programs can be adapted to fit a variety of institutional needs (Dodge et al., 2018; Garrett & Lurie, 2016). Thus, although CBE can be applied to a wide array of disciplines, the current tendency is to use CBE in fields with workforce licensure requirements and established standards (Parsons et al., 2016). As Parsons et al. (2016) write, "there is no single way to offer CBE; each program [is] unique to its institutional contexts and origins of program development" (p. 9). In addition, CBE programs may vary substantially in several key ways (Garrett & Lurie, 2016; Kelchen, 2015; Long, 2017; Parsons et al., 2016; Smither et al., 2016).

Furthermore, these characteristics may vary by program within an institution or even by course within a program. As Parsons et al. (2016) observe, there are inherent trade-offs and incentives for CBE programs in each of these variations. For example, they note that students in programs that charge tuition by course or competency cannot save financially regardless of how quickly they finish the program, whereas those in programs using a subscription model that charges a fixed price per time period can realize

Figure I.2. Competency-based education framework continuum.

Course-based, term-based, credit-hour-based competencies defined in single courses	No courses, no terms, no credit hours with competencies defined at credential level
Learning measured by seat time (credits) and assessed by classroom instructor	Learning measured by direct assessment of competency with authentic, transparent, and aligned assessment

From *A Leader's Guide to Competency-Based Education: From Inception to Implementation* by L. Dodge, D. J. Bushway, & C. S. Long, 2018, Stylus, p. 128.

substantial savings by accelerating their coursework. Thus, scholars tend to view the CBE features along a spectrum, rather than as an either-or typology. For example, Dodge et al. (2018) describe a continuum of CBE programs (Figure I.2) where leaders can pick and choose components that best meet their institutional context and needs.

It should be recognized that the federal statute currently does not offer a standardized definition of CBE; however, this work is currently underway. There are a variety of definitions being used for "competency-based" in both education and the workforce. Because of evolving data in this field, there is not one right way to build a program. The authors caution you to be wary if anyone professes that one way is the only way to build a program. The build of your program is dependent on the learners you serve, what your goals are for the program, what features you choose to adopt, what resources are available, and so forth. As you can see, there is a great deal of model variety based on the needs of the learners and the employers who hire them.

While there is variation related to how CBE is defined, there is also variety in how institutions of higher education design and offer CBE programs. In earlier years, CBE initiatives tended to share four common features, including competencies describing requisite knowledge, skills, and dispositions (often referred to as intellectual behaviors); use of assessments to measure competency acquisition; advancement based on demonstrated learning rather than seat time; and a student-centered approach (Daugherty et al., 2015; Irvine & Kevan, 2016; Phillips & Schneider, 2016). More recently, these four common features were given additional granularity as defined through eight common features of CBE initiatives shared by Deb Bushway in 2018 to the U.S. Senate Committee on Health, Education,

Labor, and Pensions. They were then reshared by Charla Long in 2019 to the U.S. House Committee on Education and Labor. These eight common features are highlighted in many programs; some contain all features, while others contain only a portion. Programs often consider these eight features for inclusion:

> *Intentional backward design.* In CBE programs, the educational journey is designed with the end in mind and the student at the center. Faculty begin by answering the question: "What ought a graduate of this program know and be able to do?" From this starting point, teams of faculty members, employers, and instructional designers develop a set of clearly specified competencies that illustrate what the learner must know and be able to do in order to progress in and complete a credential. These competencies are integrated and scaffolded so that the integrity of the academic credential is maintained.
>
> *Outcomes emphasis.* CBE is an approach to teaching and learning that focuses on the competencies that students must master rather than the amount of time they have spent in class, as measured by credit hours. This allows students with some existing knowledge or skill to spend their time on new content rather than reviewing already mastered material.
>
> *Agnostic regarding learning source.* Because well-defined competencies mandate the integration of knowledge (theory) and practice (application), CBE programs can be agnostic as to the source of students' learning. A student may have learned the practice or application component of a competency in a work setting and the theoretical component in a traditional classroom, but what matters is the student's ability to knit this together and demonstrate the competency as required by the credential being earned. The institution enrolling the student and offering the credential must provide the student with proactive, relevant, and substantive educational support that leads to this demonstrated learning.
>
> *Rigorous requirements.* Many people wrongly assume that CBE programs are easier or shorter, but in reality, a high-quality CBE program offers a very rigorous instructional model in which students must demonstrate the acquisition of *all* the competency sets required to master a program of study. In fact, for some students, CBE programs will take longer to complete than traditionally structured programs. But a high-quality CBE

program will *guarantee* the learning outcomes or competencies of the students, unlike most traditional programs.

Students at the center. In CBE programs, the student educational journey becomes a primary organizing principle. Rather than enrolling in a series of courses taught by individual faculty members, the CBE student is engaged in a carefully designed set of learning experiences and assessments built to allow the student to demonstrate the required competencies when she or he is ready to do so.

Modularization. Rather than relying on the traditional method of clustering chunks of learning into a "course," CBE disaggregates courses based on competencies demonstrated as a result of learning. Each competency is clearly articulated, and demonstration of each competency is assessed and transcribed. Modularization not only allows for more transparency, it also supports stacking of competencies into diverse credentials.

Personalization. Such modularization allows for more precision and personalization in developing the student learning journey. For each student, the path to a credential can be customized by acknowledging where competencies already exist and "prescribing" additional learning where competency is absent or incomplete.

Transparency. Student learning outcomes, or competencies, are clearly articulated and transparently transcribed so that students, employers, and the public can all know what any given credential means. This is much more meaningful than the traditional "grade" offered for a course.

In high quality CBE programs, these features are interwoven to produce value for the students in unique ways, including increased transparency of learning outcomes, potential lower costs of both tuition and time for some students, and the ability to personalize each student's learning pathway with increased precision and intentionality (*Reauthorizing the Higher Education Act*, 2018).

Such features individually and holistically contribute to the effectiveness and fit of CBE programs that serve a variety of learner populations. In a desire to protect against bad actors—institutions that might window dress efforts to be competency-based without the heavy lift of what it takes to build one—the field worked through C-BEN in 2017 to create a quality framework. The C-BEN quality framework is designed to ensure elements such as those described previously are reflected in high-quality programs.

Competency-Based Credential Design Examples

It is common for terms such as "competencies" and other related language to be used differently across programs and become a barrier to progress. An essential step for addressing this challenge before continuing with this work is to create a shared language that will support your success. Terms such as *competency* should be defined and agreed upon in order to work together toward common goals. It should be noted that the two program examples provided throughout this book used differing lexicons during the build and implementation of their respective programs. However, for the purposes of writing this book and in an effort to share the CDPM with key steps for building an effective competency-based program, a common lexicon was agreed upon for reader clarity. Figure I.3 shows the agreed upon lexicon for the purposes of this book and sharing the CDPM.

These two case studies and the agreed-upon lexicon will be used throughout the book to contextualize the CDPM. The CDPM is introduced with unique features that emphasize the interdependence of competencies, assessments, and a robust learning journey within a fully developed career pathway. Our CDPM is rooted in the knowledge and experiences of other groups, including higher education and industry, that have undertaken similar pathway design efforts. We (the authors of this book) propose using competencies as a problem-solving tool to create a clearly defined, well-articulated, accessible career pathway inclusive of postsecondary education, credentialing, and professional development systems. There are seven steps of the CDPM model:

- Step 1: Define the Pathway Problem
- Step 2: Establish the Competency Framework
- Step 3: Draft Competency Statements
- Step 4: Establish Competency Measurability
- Step 5: Develop Competency Assessments
- Step 6: Adopt and Implement Competencies in Learning Journey and Credentialing Systems
- Step 7: Evaluate the Impact of Competencies Over Time and Support Competency Sustainability

Embedded throughout this process are specific opportunities to garner expert and constituent input for the purposes of refining competencies and fully integrating them across credentialing and related professional and workforce development systems.

Figure I.3. Illinois ECE and Tennessee LTSS competency lexicon.

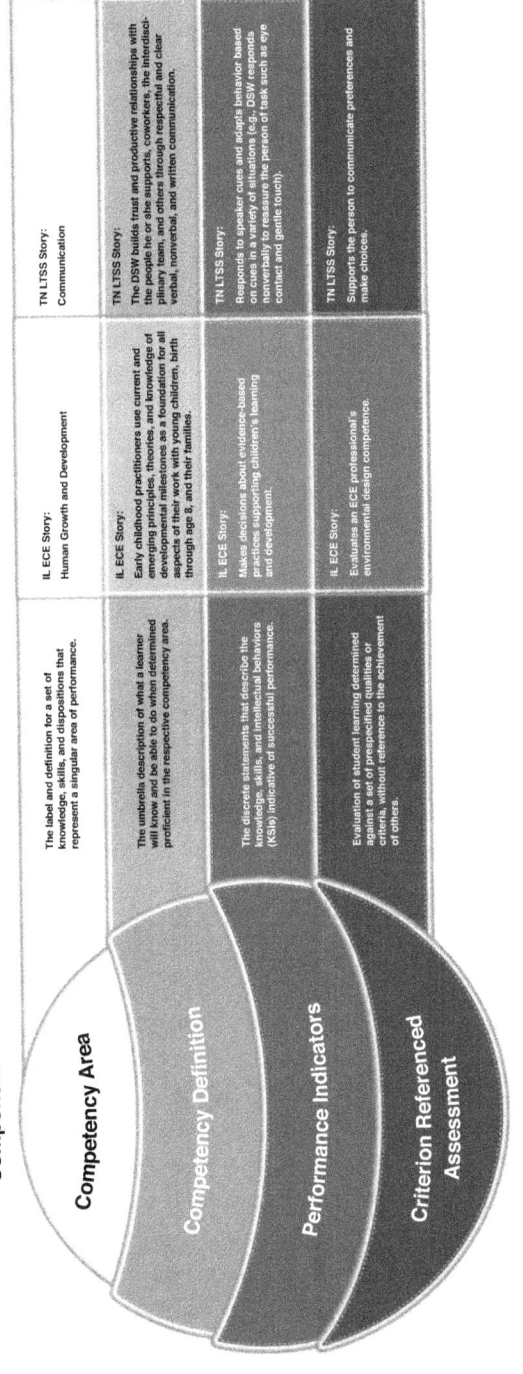

Our CDPM addresses the importance of situating competencies within a professional learning context using a backward design approach. Most importantly, our model includes iterative processes with "nearly simultaneous" consideration of assessment practices as the competency areas are being defined and the performance indicators are being developed, and it includes vetting procedures to test the competencies both for authenticity in relation to professional standards and employer expectations, and for viability in assessing attainment of competencies. In doing so, the model aims to elevate the work of designing competencies from merely developing a list of expectations to in-depth analysis and design, with the goal of developing competencies that can be readily used for assessment and career pathway development. Let's take a closer look at each step of the CDPM.

CDPM: Step 1

The central question for CDPM Step 1 is "What specific workforce development and career pathway challenges will competencies address?" Although there are a wide variety of CBE/CBL programs, they all share several design elements in common, including: identifying clear, cross-cutting, and specialized competencies; designing a competency-driven curriculum; creating meaningful assessments to measure competencies; engaging external partners; aligning professional and regulatory systems; and embedding processes for continuous improvement (Long, 2017). The career pathways approach is one strategy that many regions, industries, and postsecondary institutions have implemented to address this process systematically. This approach focuses on systems change to reorient existing education and workforce programs from a myriad of disconnected services to a clear sequence of coursework and credentials with embedded and employer-validated competencies (Alliance for Quality Career Pathways [AQCP], 2014; Manhattan Strategy Group, 2015).

According to the AQCP (2014), career pathways include:

- multiple entry and exit points leading to credentials at successively higher levels within a specific sector (or across related sectors)
- a shared vision for building, scaling, and sustaining career pathways
- engagement of employers and workers in partnership
- collaboration to identify, prioritize, and leverage resources
- policies that support systems, partners, and programs
- the use of data and shared measures to demonstrate and improve outcomes

The Workforce Innovation and Opportunity Act, the federal government's primary workforce development program, codifies these essential elements of career pathways into law, and the Illinois Workforce Innovation Board (2017) has proposed guidance for the state's career pathways programs that reflects these components.

Career pathways are designed to connect education and employment systems into an aligned and transparent system that optimizes the potential for success by helping (a) individuals earn marketable credentials, (b) industries improve the quality of the workforce, and (c) communities grow their economies (AQCP, 2014). Career pathway programs are often targeted toward underrepresented or nontraditional student populations, such as English language learners and unemployed or underemployed adults. In fact, proponents of career pathways argue that this approach is most beneficial for underrepresented and nontraditional students because they are the populations for whom educational and career success is most often impeded by the disconnect between the education and employment systems (AQCP, 2014).

The first step in career pathway design involves identifying core competencies and organizing them into a logical sequence intended to help students acquire the knowledge and skills needed to gain employment, succeed in the workplace, and progress in their careers. This package of knowledge and skills comprises the curriculum of competency-based coursework and serves as the building block for career pathways and lattices (Manhattan Strategy Group, 2015). Beyond traditional academic competencies, this package also often includes noncognitive skills and knowledge specific to a workplace or industry that is relevant to on-the-job performance (Burnette, 2016; Manhattan Strategy Group, 2015). According to the Manhattan Strategy Group (2015), embedding industry-wide skills used across sectors makes it possible for program completers to move easily across roles rather than being locked into a single career path. Further, a competency-based curriculum allows for multiple entry and exit points and often accounts for prior learning, thus allowing flexibility to meet varying student needs and goals. Lastly, work-based learning opportunities such as co-op programs, internships, apprenticeships, and third-party assessments to measure competencies are also common in career pathways programs.

A key tenet (as illustrated in Figure 1.4) in career pathways design involves shifting the role of employers from *customers* of education programs to that of *coleaders* and *coinvestors* in workforce development (Manhattan Strategy Group, 2015). Employers have long been involved with identifying competencies, and their involvement in curriculum design is crucial for validating

Figure I.4. Steps in career pathway progress.

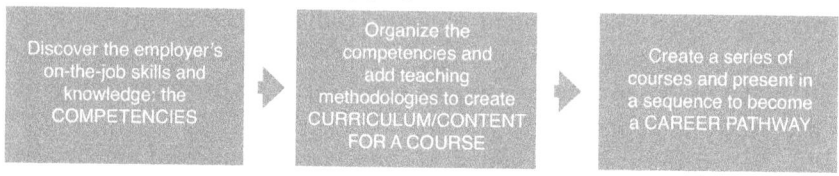

From *Career Pathways Toolkit: A Guide for System Development* by Manhattan Strategy Group, 2015, p. 43. Reprinted with permission.

competency models (Irvine & Kevan, 2016; Manhattan Strategy Group, 2015). As Camacho and Legare (2016) note, the long-term viability and credibility of CBE programs is closely linked with employers' acceptance of these competencies. A curriculum that is aligned with workforce requirements is also necessary to ensure completers master marketable skills and are familiar with modern technologies and procedures to meet the changing demands of employers (Camacho & Legare, 2016; Carnavale et al., 2017). Employers also have strong incentives to invest in the development of career pathways to provide both a steady supply of qualified workers and affordable ways to extend job-training options (Irvine & Kevan, 2016; Manhattan Strategy Group, 2015). Further, continued relationships between education and employment sectors and continuously reviewing (and modifying) competencies can ensure that the curriculum adjusts with changes in professional standards, meets labor market needs, and is responsive to unique requirements for local employers (Carnavale et al., 2017; Manhattan Strategy Group, 2015).

After this vetting process, education programs continue to engage employers throughout the program development phase (Burnette, 2016). To do this, education institutions must analyze their own capacity with regard to space, staffing, and expertise; continue collaborating with employers to identify target populations; and coordinate recruitment strategies (Manhattan Strategy Group, 2015). Career pathways programs may also provide financial, academic, and employment assistance to support students in their educational and career decision-making (Carnavale et al., 2017; Manhattan Strategy Group, 2015; Nodin & Johnstone, 2015). Pathway models are then linked with industry-recognized credentials, which are often aligned with a career lattice that describes the competencies and pathways required for individuals to ascend to higher level jobs within a particular industry (Manhattan Strategy Group, 2015).

CDPM: Step 2

The central question for CDPM Step 2 is "How should the standards, regulations, and best practices that guide the field inform development of the competency framework?" Competencies are defined as learning targets that describe what students should be able to do as a result of their learning, inclusive of knowledge, skills, and dispositions (often referred to as intellectual behaviors; Council of Regional Accrediting Commissions, 2015; Haynes et al., 2016; Long, 2017). The literature on competency development emphasizes that competencies need to be clear, specific, measurable, and transferable to other degree pathways (Haynes et al., 2016; Irvine & Kevan, 2016). According to Adelman (2013), "Competencies are not wish lists: they are learned, enhanced, expanded; they mark empirical performance, and a competency statement either directly—or at a slant—posits a documented execution" (para. 21). Competencies within a field or profession are typically defined through partnerships between higher education faculty and administration, industry leaders, and workforce representatives (Education Commission of the States, 2017). Alignment between education and workforce requires institutions of higher education to consider a best practice employer definition of competence. In a workforce setting, "competency" is defined as behavioral performance. More specifically, Washington and Griffiths (2015) and Morel and Griffiths (2018) explain that "an individual competency describes a specific set of behaviors or performance indicators associated with a facet of exceptional performance in an organizational role" (p. 11). See Figure I.5.

When a primary goal of CBE is to serve as a bridge between what employers want and what higher education provides, academic programs must consider an employer definition of competency. This has been captured in the field of education through a shared language of *competency* as the ability to apply or use a set of related knowledge, skills, abilities, and intellectual behaviors required to successfully perform tasks in a defined setting (Bushway et al., 2018). See Figure I.6.

CDPM: Step 3

The central question for CDPM Step 3 is "Based on the analysis in Step 2, what knowledge, skills, and intellectual behaviors are necessary for successful performance in the workplace role?" At the heart of CBE/CBL, and making the previous features relevant, are meaningful competencies. Identifying the right set of competencies for an employment role is key to driving quality curriculum design for a CBE program and respective teaching units. CBE programs rely on building with the end in mind, answering the key question "What should the learner know and be able to do?" See Figure I.7 for the backward design process.

Stage 1 of backward design requires the identification of a relevant competency set, comprised of multiple competencies, with corresponding

Figure I.5. A simple representation of the concept of competency.

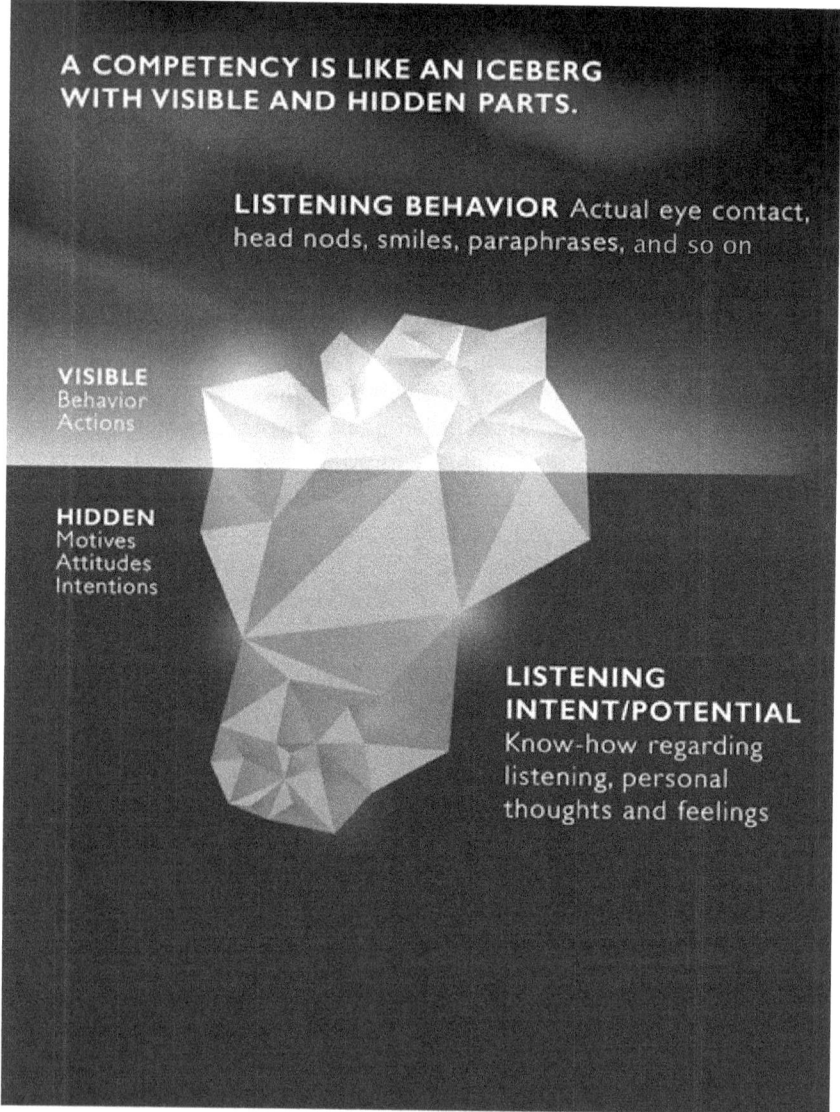

From *Redefining Competency-Based Education: Competence for Life* by N. J. Morel & B. Griffiths, 2018, Business Expert Press, p. 12.

behavioral definitions of performance, referred to as performance indicators. Stage 2 of backward design requires the plan for competency evaluation and how each competency will be appropriately measured. Stage 3 of backward design requires the build of a learning journey that explicitly builds the

Figure I.6. Graphic representation of a competency.

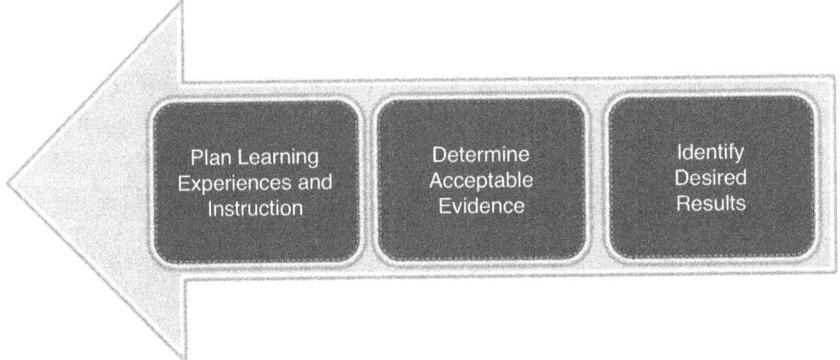

Knowledge	Skills and Abilities	Intellectual Behaviors	Application and Transfer
What does the learner need to know?	What does the learner need to be able to do?	What dispositions does the learner need to display?	Where will the learner apply these competencies and at what level?

From *A Leaders' Guide to Competency-Based Education: From Inception to Implementation* by D. Bushway, L. Dodge, & C. Long, 2018, p. 1.

Figure I.7. The backward design process.

Plan Learning Experiences and Instruction → Determine Acceptable Evidence → Identify Desired Results

From C-BEN, (n.d.).

learner to successful demonstration of each competency. By starting with the end in mind, you are able to offer learners a clear and relevant pathway to successful performance.

CDPM: Step 4

The central question for CDPM Step 4 is "How will you know competence when you see it?" Once competencies have been developed, CBE programs use assessments to measure whether students have met learning targets and can apply their knowledge in different situations, and to determine if they may advance to subsequent levels (Burnette, 2016; Klein-Collins, 2013). CBE programs use common, consistent, and criterion-referenced summative assessments in order to apply the same standards to all students and to ensure test results mean the same thing from course to course; thus, programs and schools can certify that students have acquired competencies (Long, 2017; Malan, 2000; Worthen & Pace, 2014). Some research on CBE assessment suggests that multiple measures should be used to determine mastery, and that assessments ought to be robust, meaningful, and authentic for learners (C-BEN, 2017; Le et al., 2014). Formative assessments also typically play an important role in CBE programs, allowing students to understand which competencies they have yet to master and providing time to practice these concepts and skills until they can demonstrate proficiency (C-BEN, 2021; Haynes et al., 2016; Le et al., 2014). Most importantly, discrete indicators of successful performance should be articulated and used as criteria to evaluate and determine proficient demonstration of competence.

CDPM: Step 5

The central question for CDPM Step 5 is "What is the evidence of competence?" CBE programs provide credit on the basis of mastering learning expectations, rather than the traditional measures of credit hours or seat time (Daugherty et al., 2015; Dodge et al., 2018; Haynes et al., 2016; Irvine & Kevan, 2016; Kelchen, 2015; Klein-Collins, 2013; Laitinen, 2012; Malan, 2000; Mallett, 2016). In a CBE model, students cannot advance until they have demonstrated the knowledge and skills outlined by a set of competencies. In comparison, students in the traditional credit-hour model advance based on completion of the course requirements within the scheduled time frame and not necessarily their mastery of all course objectives or standards (Camacho & Legare, 2016; Le et al., 2014). That is, as Long (2017) describes, in the traditional credit-hour model, time is fixed but learning is variable, whereas in the CBE model, time is variable but learning is fixed. In other words, a demonstration of competence is required.

CDPM: Step 6

The central question for CDPM Step 6 is "What processes will be needed to anchor competencies in education and workforce contexts?" This step focuses on the build of an effective learning journey and how to deliver the learner to successful performance of the competency areas. This build includes considering features such as modularization or pacing. For example, Lurie et al. (2019) explain learner pacing as focused on learning outcomes as opposed to synchronous course minutes allowing students to work through learning targets at their own pace outside of traditional academic calendar restrictions. Many CBE programs also use personalized or adaptive instruction, often via online course delivery, to ensure that students receive timely and challenging support to match their individual learning needs and that they will be able to reach proficiency (Burnette, 2016; CAEL, 2015; Daugherty et al., 2015; Haynes et al., 2016; Klein-Collins, 2013; Le et al., 2014; Long, 2017; Worthen & Pace, 2014). These optional features are decisions that need to be made in order to anchor competencies in education and workforce contexts with features that best support the learners of the respective program.

CDPM: Step 7

The central question for CDPM Step 7 is "So what? Did competencies make a difference?" This step focuses on the evaluation of competencies and their impact over time to ensure the model is what you intend for it to be. You will identify evaluation touchpoints; systematically collect data; analyze data; and review, disseminate, and use findings for program improvement and field growth. Data is often three-pronged as it is used to monitor learner progress and growth, create an instructor–learner feedback loop, and inform a continuous improvement process.

Navigating the Model

As you work your way through this book, each step of the CDPM will be outlined, two examples will be provided, and lastly, an opportunity for you to think about the step through your own context will be offered. Navigational beacons will help you find your way through each step (chapter). Each step in the CDPM is treated as a chapter. For each step, we identify the central question that must be answered, provide an overview of the tasks in the step, and illustrate the steps in action through examples from the Illinois ECE and Tennessee LTSS stories as described previously. Each step concludes with "Your Turn"—workbook-style guiding questions for the reader to apply the information to their particular context.

 The Steps of the Model

This icon will indicate in each step a narrative explanation/overview of that step in the model. A central question answered by the step will be provided along with a detailed description of the step and how it builds from the previous step.

Remodeling the House: The Illinois ECE Story

This icon will indicate the first of our two examples in each step. Our Illinois ECE example will describe how the step was carried out in our Illinois journey to move the system credentialing early childhood teachers and professionals in the state to a competency-based system. We used this "remodeling the house" header and icon because the Illinois journey involved taking an existing credentialing benchmark set, process, and system and "remodeling" it to incorporate a competency model. In these example vignettes you will see that the bones of the structure were there, and they were retained in the competency work.

 Building From a Blueprint: The Tennessee LTSS Story

This icon and header will indicate our second example in each step. This example will describe the step through the lens of the preparation and professional development of long-term care professionals in Tennessee. The "blueprint" icon and header were chosen because this example showcases the development of a competency-based system based on established professional standards (the blueprint), but where no system or structure previously existed.

 Your Turn

Lastly in each chapter you will be given the opportunity to walk through a series of exercises and questions to examine the step in deeper ways, using your specific context and competency goals. Our goal is that "your turns" will assist you as you launch your own competency journey.

References

Adelman, C. (2013, June 6). Competence, technology, and their discontents. *Inside Higher Ed.* http://www.insidehighered.com/views/2013/06/06/higher-ed-discovers-competency-again-essay

Alliance for Quality Career Pathways. (2014, June). *Shared vision, strong systems: The Alliance for Quality Career Pathways framework version 1.0.* CLASP. https://www.clasp.org/wp-content/uploads/2022/01/AQCP-Framework.pdf

Book, P. A. (2014). *All hands on deck: Ten lessons from early adopters of competency-based education.* Western Interstate Commission for Higher Education. http://files.eric.ed.gov/fulltext/ED546830.pdf

Burnette, D. M. (2016). The renewal of competency-based education: A review of the literature. *Journal of Continuing Higher Education, 64*(2), 84–93. https://doi.org/10.1080/07377363.2016.1177704

Bushway, D., Dodge, L., & Long, C. (2018). *A leaders' guide to competency-based education: From inception to implementation.* Stylus.

Camacho, D. J., & Legare, J. M. (2016). Shifting gears in the classroom—movement toward personalized learning and competency-based education. *The Journal of Competency-Based Education, 1*(4), 151–156. https://doi.org/10.1002/cbe2.1032

Carnavale, A. P., Garcia, T. I., & Gulish, A. (2017). *Career pathways: Five ways to connect college and careers.* Georgetown University Center on Education and the Workforce.

Center for Law and Social Policy. (2015). *Funding career pathways: A federal funding toolkit for state and local/regional career pathway partnerships.* https://www.clasp.org/sites/default/files/publications/2017/04/Career-Pathways-Funding-Toolkit-2015-8_0.pdf

Competency-Based Education Network. (n.d.). *Competency-based education.* https://www.cbenetwork.org/competency-based-education/

Competency-Based Education Network. (2017). *Quality framework for competency-based education programs.* https://www.cbenetwork.org/wp-content/uploads/2018/09/1st_button_CBE17016__Quality_Framework_Update.pdf

Competency-Based Education Network. (2021). *Hallmark practices in CBE Assessment.* https://www.cbenetwork.org/wp-content/uploads/2022/03/CBE-2021-Hallmark-Practices-WEB.pdf

Connecting Credentials. (2017). *A guide to using the beta credentials framework: A universal credentials translator.* http://connectingcredentials.org/wp-content/uploads/2017/10/CC_User-Guide_v6.pdf

Council for Adult and Experiential Learning. (2015). *Competency-based education and quality assurance.* http://cdn2.hubspot.net/hubfs/617695/CAEL_Reports/2014_CBE_Convening_Findings_Report.pdf

Council of Regional Accrediting Commissions. (2015, June 2). *Statement of the Council of Regional Accrediting Commissions (C-RAC) framework for competency-based education* [Press release]. https://www.insidehighered.com/sites/default/server_files/files/C-RAC%20CBE%20Statement%20Press%20Release%206_2.pdf

Daugherty, L., Davis, V. L., & Miller, T. (2015). *Competency-based education programs in Texas: An innovative approach to higher education.* RAND Corporation. http://www.rand.org/pubs/research_reports/RR1239-1.html

Dodge, L., Bushway, D. J., & Long, C. S. (2018). *A leader's guide to competency-based education: From inception to implementation.* Stylus.

Education Commission of the States. (2017, June). *Policy snapshot: Competency-based education.* http://www.ecs.org/ec-content/uploads/PS-Competency-Based-Education.pdf

Fain, P. (2014, October 28). Big Ten and the next big thing. *Inside Higher Ed.* https://www.insidehighered.com/news/2014/10/28/competency-based-education-arrives-three-major-public-institutions

Ganzglass, E., Bird, K., & Prince, H. (2011). *Giving credit where credit is due: Creating a competency-based qualifications framework for postsecondary education and training*. Center for Law and Social Policy (CLASP). https://www.clasp.org/publications/report/brief/giving-credit-where-credit-due-creating-competency-based-qualifications

Garrett, R., & Lurie, H. (2016). *Deconstructing CBE: An assessment of institutional activity, goals, and challenges in higher education*. Lumina Foundation. https://www.luminafoundation.org/files/resources/deconstructing-cbe.pdf

Haynes, E., Zeiser, K., Surr, W., Hauser, A., Clymer, L., Walston, J., Bitter, C., & Yang, R. (2016). *Looking under the hood of competency-based education: The relationship between competency-based education practices and students' learning skills, behaviors, and dispositions*. Nellie Mae Education Foundation. https://www.air.org/sites/default/files/downloads/report/CBE-Study%20Full%20Report.pdf

Illinois Workforce Innovation Board (2017). *Illinois common career pathways definition and guidance*. https://www.illinoisworknet.com/DownloadPrint/8R%20%20request%20to%20Approve%20CP%20Definition%20final.pdf

Irvine, C. K. S., & Kevan, J. M. (2016). Competency-based education in higher education. In K. Rasmussen, P. Northrup, & R. Colson (Eds.), *Handbook of research on competency-based education in university settings* (pp. 1–27). IGI Global.

Kelchen, R. (2015). *The landscape of competency-based education: Enrollments, demographics, and affordability*. American Enterprise Institute for Public Policy Research. http://files.eric.ed.gov/fulltext/ED566651.pdf

Klein-Collins, R. (2013, November). *Sharpening our focus on learning: The rise of competency-based approaches to degree completion*. National Institute for Learning Outcomes Assessment.

Le, C., Wolfe, R. E., & Steinberg, A. (2014). *The past and the promise: Today's competency education movement*. Students at the Center: Competency Education Research Series. Jobs for the Future. https://files.eric.ed.gov/fulltext/ED561253.pdf

Lumina Foundation for Education. (2015). *Connecting credentials: Making the case for reforming the U.S. credentialing system*. https://www.luminafoundation.org/files/resources/making-the-case.pdf

Lurie, H., Mason, J., & Parsons, K. (2019). State of the field: Findings from the 2018 National Survey of Postsecondary Competency-Based Education (NSPCBE). American Institutes for Research.

Malan, S. (2000). The "new paradigm" of outcomes-based education in perspective. *Tydskrif vir Gesinsekologie en Verbruikerswetenskappe, 28*, 22–28. http://wings.buffalo.edu/ubtlc/resources/Outcomes-based_education.pdf

Mallett, C. (2016). *A study of postsecondary competency-based education practices in the context of disruptive innovation theory* [Doctoral dissertation, Pepperdine University]. ProQuest LLC. http://search.proquest.com/docview/1807951046

Manhattan Strategy Group. (2015). *Career pathways toolkit: A guide for system development*. U.S. Department of Labor. https://wdr.doleta.gov/directives/attach/TEN/TEN_17-15_Attachment_Acc.pdf

McClarty, K. L., & Gaertner, M. N. (2015). *Measuring mastery: Best practices for assessment in competency-based education*. American Enterprise Institute for Public Policy Research.

McCombs, B. L., & Vakili, D. (2005). A learner-centered framework for e-learning. *Teachers College Record, 107*(8), 1582–1600.

Morel, N. J., & Griffiths, B. (2018). *Redefining competency based education: Competence for life*. Business Expert Press.

Nodin, T., & Johnstone, S. (2015). CBE programs promote productive business partnerships. *Community College Week, 27*, 8. https://ccweekblog.wordpress.com/

Ohio Department of Higher Education. (2016). *Competency-based education: 9th report on the condition of higher education in Ohio*. http://files.eric.ed.gov/fulltext/ED572750.pdf

Parsons, K., Mason, J., & Soldner, M. (2016). *On the path to success: Early evidence about the efficacy of postsecondary competency-based education programs*. American Institutes for Research.

Phillips, K., & Schneider, C. (2016). *Policy, pilots, and the path to competency-based education: A tale of three states*. ExcelinEd. https://www.excelined.org/wp-content/uploads/FEIE_TaleOf3States-20Sep2016.pdf

Porter, S. R. (2016). Competency-based education and federal student aid. *Journal of Student Financial Aid, 46*(3), Article 2. http://publications.nasfaa.org/jsfa/vol46/iss3/2/

Porto, S. (2013). Cost, access, and quality: Breaking the iron triangle through disruptive technology-based innovations. In K. Shattuck (Ed.), *Assuring quality in online education: Practices and processes at the teaching, resource, and program levels* (pp. 18–39). Stylus.

Reauthorizing the higher education act: Access and innovation, 115th Cong. (2018) (testimony of Deborah Bushway). https://www.help.senate.gov/hearings/reauthorizing-the-higher-education-act-access-and-innovation

Smither, C., Parsons, K., Peek, A., & Soldner, M. (2016, August). *Key characteristics of postsecondary competency-based education programs: A descriptive rubric*. American Institutes for Research. http://www.air.org/sites/default/files/downloads/report/Descriptive%20CBE%20Rubric%20v20160819.pdf

Walters, G. (2016). Developing competency-based advising practices in response to paradigm shifts in higher education. *NACADA Journal, 3*(1), 66–79. http://files.eric.ed.gov/fulltext/EJ1115465.pdf

Washington, E., & Griffiths, B. (2015). *Competencies at work: Providing a common language for talent management*. Business Expert Press.

White House Office of the Press Secretary. (2013, August 22). *Fact sheet on the president's plan to make college more affordable: A better bargain for the middle class* [Press release]. http://www.whitehouse.gov/the-press-office/2013/08/22/fact-sheet-president-s-plan-make-college-more-affordable-better-bargain-

Worthen, M., & Pace, L. (2014). *A K–12 federal policy framework for competency education: Building capacity for systems change*. iNACOL and CompetencyWorks. http://www.competencyworks.org/wp-content/uploads/2014/01/CompetencyWorks_A_K-12_Federal_Policy_Framework_for_Competency_Education_February_2014.pdf

Step 1

DEFINE THE PATHWAY PROBLEM

Central Question: What specific workforce development and career pathway challenges will competencies address?

CBE is not a new idea, but it has received renewed attention for the possibilities it offers in terms of addressing an array of workforce development and career pathway challenges ranging from quality assurance to the iron triangle of cost, access, and quality (Dodge et al., 2018). The first step in our CDPM rests on the basic premise that competency performance indicators, no matter how thoughtfully crafted, are not in and of themselves a solution to these challenges. Readers preparing to develop CBE/CBL programs should begin their efforts with a careful examination of their own unique educational or workforce/employment contexts and identify specific workforce development or career pathway challenges contributing to gaps or disconnects in student learning, completion, or professional performance.

Well-designed career pathways can make explicit the links between educational preparation, employment opportunities, and professional progression in a field. We contend that clear, measurable, meaningful competency performance indicators are effective tools for operationalizing a career pathway and making performance expectations transparent across educational and workforce/employment contexts. CBE and CBL programs built on clear, measurable, meaningful competency performance indicators have several strengths that contribute to seamless career pathway models. In the professional development context, these strengths include:

- increased ability to provide individualized instruction, supporting academic engagement, motivation, and self-efficacy (Camacho & Legare, 2016; Dodge et al., 2018; Haynes et al., 2016)
- provision of a more affordable, flexible education model that meets the needs of nontraditional students (Garrett & Lurie, 2016)
- accessible, innovative pathways supporting college access and completion (Book, 2014; Daugherty et al., 2015)
- greater transparency, accountability, portability, and comparability of postsecondary credentials, resulting in increased access and economic mobility for traditionally underserved populations (Book, 2014; Burnette, 2016; Ganzglass et al., 2011)

There are many factors that influence the decision to create and implement a CBE/CBL model. In Step 1, we focus on identifying challenges that arise in education and workforce contexts and how competency performance indicators and related components of CBE/CBL programs can be designed in ways that address career pathway issues. This initial step of our CDPM provides exemplars focused on career pathway challenges emerging from the higher education context in Illinois and the workforce context in Tennessee.

What Challenges Related to Recruiting and Preparing Professionals Exist Within the Field?

Higher education programs are shaped by academic content and pedagogy as well as preparatory experiences that occur outside the classroom, such as practica and formal field-based training. These components are often shaped by professional standards and state licensing and certification requirements and are ideally designed to adequately prepare students for successful performance in the workforce context.

Preparation pathways include arranging academic content, pedagogy, and required field-based experience in a meaningful, streamlined way that is transparent to both the student and the employer and supportive of career pathway goals. As noted in the introduction to this book, employer concerns are another important reason for implementing competency-based programs, specifically the concern that higher education graduates lack knowledge and skills essential for successful performance in the workforce (Laitinen, 2012). Morel and Griffiths (2018) highlight higher education's focus on discipline knowledge that *should* lead to competent performance as opposed to the employers' focus on performance of a competency.

When developing competency-based programs, it is important to identify specific preparation pathway challenges that are housed within the educational context. These challenges can be evidenced by several factors, including:

- low institutional retention rates
- a lack of student degree or credential completion
- excessive credit hour attainment in the pursuit of targeted degrees or credentials
- overidentification of students for placement in developmental education programs or coursework
- extended time and cost for transfer students completing degrees/credentials (Jenkins & Fink, 2015; Monaghan & Attewell, 2014)

Clear, measurable, meaningful statements of competency and well-designed CBE/CBL programs can be a quality assurance that supports student understanding of content (Long, 2017) and the ability to appropriately apply the information in professional settings (Ganzglass et al., 2011). Career preparation pathway challenges in the previously outlined areas may be indicative of challenges related to transparency or accountability. The backward design features of competency-based programs promote improved transparency related to expected knowledge, skills, and dispositions as well as accountability for demonstrating the same (Lumina Foundation, 2015). For example, a lack of degree completion and/or excessive credit hour attainment may reflect a lack of transparency.

What Challenges Related to Workforce Participation, Performance, and Persistence Exist?

Once students in professional preparation programs complete a credential or degree, pathway problems within workforce contexts can be evidenced by several factors, including:

- failure to obtain a position in the intended career field
- low rates of persistence in the intended career field
- a lack of demonstration of required knowledge and skills within the workplace
- difficulty in career pathway progression, based on education attainment (Darragh Ernst et al., 2016)

How these challenges in the workforce context manifest themselves will depend on the specific field. Designers of competency-based programs need to pay careful attention to the range of workforce roles and levels of performance expected within those roles, the knowledge and skills required for employment, and how employment requirements are aligned and represented. It is also important to consider the developmental needs of individuals likely to seek employment within the field and how preparation programs provide options and opportunities for students to attain the knowledge and skills needed to perform targeted roles. Attention to these factors, and the resulting intentional backward design, creates deep reciprocity between preparation and workforce contexts. Cohesive, flexible preparation pathways support a successful transition into workforce settings. These pathways further support advanced professional opportunities, including higher level employment positions within the field or deeper professional development in the current employment role.

The examples provided highlight two CBE/CBL build program processes described by Bushway et al. (2018), each case answering the question "What should students know, understand, and be able to do at the end of the program?" As described in the introduction, the Illinois early childhood CBL approach (referred to as "Remodeling the House") is one of deconstruction-reconstruction, which included the deconstruction of existing learning outcomes, relevant standards, and regulations and the construction of a revised, streamlined framework based on new groupings of learning and competency sequences. The Tennessee LTSS approach (referred to as "Building From a Blueprint") is one of framework origin, which included the build of a CBE program based on relevant frameworks, standards, databases, industry standard certifications, and so on, by beginning with the end in mind.

 Remodeling the House: The Illinois ECE Story

The CDPM emerged from our work to address pathway problems in the field of early childhood education (ECE) in the state of Illinois. Multiple agencies in Illinois regulate professional requirements for employment in early childhood care and education, including the Department of Children and Family Services (DCFS), the Illinois Department of Human Services (IDHS), the Illinois State Board of Education (ISBE), and Head Start under the auspices of the U.S. Department of Health and Human Services (HHS). Individuals preparing for careers in the Illinois ECE system must navigate disparate requirements for licensure and employment based on administrative rules set by each of these agencies. There are differing and disconnected professional preparation mandates represented in these administrative rules, resulting in pathway challenges within and between educational and workforce settings—an issue that is true for the ECE field nationally. Because of vastly different professional mandates, the answer to the question "What ought a graduate of this program know and be able to do?" is varied and vague.

Consequently, adults seeking a career in ECE must choose a specific educational pathway or degree program based on the administrative rules of the agency regulating employment in that setting. This disconnect results in barriers to mobility in terms of employment options and professional advancement within the field. Table 1.1 provides an example of this disparity related to the role of teaching assistants in the early childhood field. The disparity exemplified in this table extends to additional roles in the field.

As noted earlier, effective career pathways are defined by clear expectations of and transparent routes to the knowledge and skills required for specific roles within the field. In Illinois, varied employment requirements across state agencies resulted in a broken career pathway in the field of ECE, presenting challenges in both the workforce and educational contexts. The Illinois Gateways to Opportunity credentialing system has been instrumental in improving the career pathway and developing a more highly educated early childhood workforce in Illinois licensed child-care settings; 71% of ECE workers hold associate or baccalaureate degrees, compared to the national average of 53% (Illinois Network of Child Care Resource and Referral Agencies [INCCRRA], 2014; Schilder, 2016). Despite the successes of the Gateways credentialing system in supporting a more cohesive career pathway, data from the Illinois Gateways to Opportunity Registry indicates pathway complications in student degree and credential completion.

TABLE 1.1

Early Childhood Education Role by Educational Requirements: Teaching Assistant

Role	DCFS Licensing Requirements	Gateways ECE Level 2 Credential Requirements	ISBE Requirements
Teaching Assistant	High School Diploma or GED Equivalent	**Level 2** 16 college credit hours (12-hour ECE requirement) AND 10 hours of observation within an ECE classroom	30 college credit hours in any field

The Illinois Gateways to Opportunity Registry is used to track attainment of courses, credentials, degrees, and training for individuals across diverse program settings in the early childhood field. Despite over a decade of statewide investment supporting the educational attainment and career development of individuals pursuing careers in ECE or currently working in the field, 2014 Illinois Gateways Registry data indicate that of those who have attained degrees and credentials, 75% of early childhood teachers, 32% of assistants, and 85% of ECE center directors lacked formal content knowledge specific to child development and ECE (INCCRRA, 2014). These data confirm that many in the field lack a credential or degree specific to ECE despite credit hours attained.

Challenges in degree and credential completion can relate to transparency (not understanding needed pathways or what credential/degree attainment means), accountability (a failure of programs to create pathways leading to completion), or even portability (students swirling from program to program without courses transferring). Illinois publications funded through Race to the Top funds and guided by the Illinois Board of Higher Education provided a faculty lens that further clarified and supported understanding of field-based pathway problems and potential solutions. Some of the most pressing issues identified by faculty within these publications included:

- a lack of student degree or credential completion
- excessive credit hour attainment in pursuit of a targeted degree or credential
- difficulty in progressing through career pathways (Latorre & Batchelor, 2016; Mathien et al., 2016; McIntyre et al., 2016; Pruitt et al., 2016; Steinhaus & Walker, 2016)

Difficulty in progressing through preparation pathways, course articulation, and related transfer pathway supports was identified by Illinois ECE faculty as a critical issue in the field. While Illinois has many structures supporting strong articulation (including established transfer elements, statewide policies and practices supporting articulation, transfer data, and reporting, and a state articulation system called the Illinois Articulation Initiative), ECE courses between community colleges and universities are not always parallel (Bernoteit et al., 2016). This lack of a portable preparation pathway, inclusive of articulated courses, is a significant pathway challenge and one that served as the catalyst for our state's competency development project.

Competencies as a tool to address these challenges emerged from a partnership between one university and three feeder community colleges in

Central Illinois. Faculty within this partnership identified creating accessible, transparent pathways to support completion of ECE credentials and degrees as an initial goal in addressing the existing pathway challenges of noncompletion and excessive time and cost to degree. Early childhood faculty at these institutions viewed developing and implementing a competency-based system as one way to create seamless preparation pathways where competencies provide "a codified conceptual framework regarding what individuals working with young children need to know and be able to do" (Gomez et al., 2015, p. 178).

The initial decision of developing competencies to support intra-institutional articulation expanded to the use of competencies as tools that might address broader disconnects between educational and workforce contexts in the field of ECE across Illinois. Discussions with key state partners led to broad support for the idea that the Gateways ECE competencies could serve not only as tools to improve identified higher education transfer and articulation challenges, but also as a lever to address pathway challenges in the field of ECE across the state. In our story; clear, measurable, meaningful statements of performance provided a profound solution to a multiplicity of interacting ECE career pathway challenges. Facets of these solutions, emerging within the context of higher education, included:

- *competency-based* performance indicators embedded across the state professional development system, anchored on a behaviorally defined set of competency areas and created using the backward design process
- *demonstration* of competency through formative and summative assessments, defined within a competency-based assessment system
- validation and recognition through *industry-recognized credentials*
- *portability through a statewide registry and a transfer articulation system*, allowing opportunities for continued development and employer validation of earned credentials
- a *credit-bearing framework*
- transparency in professional and educational growth by articulating *clear career and college pathways*

Building From a Blueprint: The Tennessee LTSS Story

The competency model for the Quality Improvement in Long-Term Services and Supports Workforce Development (QuILTSS WFD) Initiative emerged from efforts to address a workforce crisis in the field of long-term services and supports (LTSS) in the state of Tennessee. The Bureau of TennCare is the state of Tennessee's Medicaid program, which provides physical and behavioral health care and LTSS for approximately 1.4 million Tennesseans, roughly 20% of the state's population. With Governor Bill Haslam's support, the Bureau of TennCare committed to designing and implementing payment reforms across LTSS programs, which serve Tennessee's most vulnerable citizens, including older adults and people with disabilities. Reimbursement reform helped to align payment with the quality of care people receive and the impact of those services on recipients' health and quality of life. TennCare's QuILTSS initiative was designed to accomplish these goals by establishing a value-based purchasing system, which is recognized as a national model. The system development was supported by the federal Centers for Medicare and Medicaid Services (CMS) through a state innovations model (SIM) test grant to help Tennessee achieve its vision.

Very early in the value-based purchasing work, TennCare recognized the critical importance of a high-quality workforce and the tremendous impact of the national workforce shortage on their ability to accomplish this goal. The shortage of workers to deliver high-quality LTSS is a multifaceted issue that is impacting states across the country, as memorialized in the *Report to the President 2017: America's Direct Support Workforce Crisis* by the President's Committee for People with Intellectual Disabilities. Among the most promising practices the report identified that would address the workforce crisis is "using competency-based training models that lead to credentialing or certification of staff and yield wage increases" (President's Committee for People with Intellectual Disabilities, 2017, p. 9). This means that effective solutions have the potential to have a broader impact far beyond the state boundaries of Tennessee.

As a result, QuILTSS was designed to improve the quality of LTSS received by the aging population and adults with disabilities through enhanced training for an expanded pipeline of qualified employees known as direct service workers (DSWs). Tennessee's 52% annual turnover rate in this field is higher than the national average and can be attributed, at least in part, to the lack of quality training and development provided to DSWs. With as many as 60,000 DSWs in Tennessee, serving both the aging population and adults with disabilities across a wide array of settings, tens of thousands of newly trained employees are needed every year.

Important to note is that the QuILTSS WFD Initiative is only one component of TennCare's broader workforce development strategy. It also includes the alignment of payment to providers and ultimately to DSWs at the individual level based in part on level of staff competence as evidenced by their successful completion of training. Incentive payments for nursing facility DSWs are embedded in the reimbursement structure set forth in administrative rules effective in 2021. There are future plans to roll out incentive payments to other LTSS providers focused around workforce recruitment and retention strategies, including competency-based training.

In addition to improving the quality of LTSS by building a more qualified workforce to provide care to Tennessee's most vulnerable residents, the workforce development initiative sought a partnership with the Tennessee Board of Regents (TBR) to increase the number of Tennesseans with a postsecondary degree or certificate to 55% by 2025. TBR is a supervising agency over a network of 40 participating community colleges and technical colleges across Tennessee. Collaboration between TBR and the Bureau of TennCare on the QuILTSS initiative has the potential to significantly impact the state of Tennessee. The QuILTSS WFD Initiative is an opportunity to align efforts around accomplishing priority educational initiatives of the governor, while at the same time significantly improving the lives of people who receive LTSS, their families, and the workforce that serves them.

Technical Assistance to the Bureau of TennCare

While confronting the state's workforce crisis in LTSS, the Bureau of TennCare desired to better understand the needs and wants of its key stakeholders, namely individuals receiving LTSS, their families, DSWs, and other community members. Intentional and focused efforts to "listen" to key stakeholders were made possible with funds awarded to Lipscomb University via a contract with Princeton University, as part of the Robert Wood Johnson Foundation's State Quality and Value Strategies (SQVS) program.

The funding award to Lipscomb University resulted in broad stakeholder review and recommendations to TennCare regarding the quality framework and implementation process. Participants were asked to rank topics in order of importance based on clinical and nonclinical categories. The pooled data showed that "consumers believe having a more well-trained workforce to be the most important in care, while providers felt making sure the workforce demonstrates dignity and caring to consumers, while providing choices to consumers in person-centered care, was most important" (Lipscomb University, n.d., p. 45). It is important to note, although the pooled data recognized different categorical areas, all areas directly relate to the workforce.

A number of themes and patterns emerged through stakeholder feedback. Key insights about provider-offered training practices at this time included the following:

- *Training is not leading to an increase in staff retention or a reduction in turnover.* In the field of LTSS, there are not enough staff to fill positions. We have more people who need LTSS than there are workers to provide these essential services. *What would happen if a well-designed, competency-based training program could lead to an increase in staff retention and a reduction in turnover?*
- *Training is being completed just to say we have completed training.* Too often, required trainings do not meet the needs of the staff, nor do they help improve on-the-job skills. One provider shared his minute-long training on abuse and neglect, and it consisted of a staff member going from person to person with a clipboard in hand to remind each employee what constitutes abuse. Then, after he finished his "training," DSWs would sign that they had been trained. *What if providers were held to a higher standard and were required to offer quality programs?*
- *Training is not consistent from provider to provider.* In the field of LTSS, each provider is often responsible for training its employees and preparing them for the workplace role. Although the same knowledge and skills are required in the field; training content, the approach, and workplace readiness are left to the devices of the individual provider. This means that training may or may not be similar across providers and the lack of standardization often leads to disparate outcomes for those served. *What if staff received consistent training across providers to better ensure quality of life and care for those served?*
- *Training is not leading to improved performance by employees.* Training content is often designed with a forward design process. In other words, a list of topics is outlined, and teaching is designed based on that list of topics. This is referred to as a "train and hope" approach, which leaves learning up to chance. Learning content is designed with the hope that it will prepare the learner for successful performance. *What if training was designed with a backward process where we explicitly and transparently identify what the DSW should know and be able to do, and then we create training programs to help DSWs build these competencies?*
- *Training lacks portability.* Individual providers are responsible for training employees and preparing them for success in the workplace.

When training is inconsistent across providers, an employee is not typically "credited" for trainings completed through a previous employer or a different employer where they may be working hours concurrently. In other words, without a system to ensure the type and quality of training an employee has previously completed, each provider must retrain each employee. *What if a high-quality consistent training program allowed DSWs to get credit for training received from one employer when working for another entity, and would this lead to lower training costs for providers?*

- *Training provided by employers lacks validation or recognition through an industry-recognized or academic credential.* Staff in the field of LTSS receive a lot of training, yet do not have a way to show they have attained specific skill sets or, at minimum, that they have completed specific trainings. For example, if a DSW completes training in a specialized area such as employment support or has specialized skills in this area, there is currently not a way for the DSW to show or communicate competence in the specialty area. *What if all training could lead to a recognized credential that allowed for progress on a postsecondary credential, which could help lift the DSW in lifetime earning potential?*

- *Training does not consistently equate to improved quality of care and quality of life for those served.* There are too many complaints and allegations about the quality of LTSS, and many of these can be substantiated as abuse, neglect, negligence, and even malpractice. There are many people receiving services and supports who regularly experience quality of support issues, which, in turn, leads to a decline in one's quality of life. *What if a person's quality of life could be improved just by better training for DSWs?*

With these questions in mind, the QuILTSS team began creating the QuILTSS WFD program to address the identified concerns. With a rough framework in mind, the QuILTSS team and TennCare officials held nine QuILTSS WFD forums around Tennessee to directly pitch to providers the competency-based training framework being leveraged, and to gather more specific information from key stakeholders. Over one thousand providers attended the forums and provided feedback.

As a part of each forum, participants completed feedback specifically related to the QuILTSS initiative through a feedback card designed with a series of open-ended questions that gathered information related to stakeholder needs. An example is: *The part(s) of the QuILTSS Workforce Development Initiative I like best is/are . . . .* Ultimately, the feedback was used to align stakeholder pressure points to the WFD training program design and curriculum.

The QuILTSS WFD Program

Key questions outlined for addressing primary challenges lead to key questions for moving toward a solution. *What if multiple organizations could collaborate to solve training challenges? How can collaboration change the experience for DSWs in the field of LTSS? How can this, in turn, change the experience, quality of services and supports received, and quality of life for persons supported?* Based on the challenges and key questions for addressing such challenges, a framework was built as a training solution: the QuILTSS WFD program, which is a CBE program designed to address the training challenges identified by key stakeholders.

Designed as a workforce solution, the QuILTSS WFD program is anchored on seven key tenets that will be described in detail in following chapters, including:

- The training is *competency-based*, as it is anchored on a behaviorally defined set of competency areas and created using the backward design process.
- The training has *required demonstration* of competency through authentic assessment, both formative and summative.
- The training will be validated and recognized through *microcredentials*.
- The training allows for *portability through a registry*, meaning DSWs' training records follow them and employers can validate earned credentials.
- The training provides wraparound *faculty, coach, and mentor support*.
- The training has a *credit-bearing framework*, allowing for training to be transcribed for college-level credit.
- The training makes professional and educational growth transparent by articulating *clear career and college pathways*.

Once a framework for the QuILTSS WFD program was defined, the QuILTSS team began to design, build, and implement a comprehensive competency-based WFD program and credentialing registry system. The QuILTSS Institute (TQI) was founded in 2018 as a nonprofit entity to exist between TennCare and academic institutions to retain program content for workforce development and other specialty areas as well as broker the relationship between state agencies. In our story, the seven key tenets undergird all CBE programs, beginning with clear, measurable, and meaningful competencies to ensure a consistent and validated training experience to benefit all key stakeholders.

Points of Intersection: Illinois and Tennessee

In our stories, the language of competency performance indicators and adoption of broader competency-based programs brought much-needed clarity and cohesion to pervasive pathway problems, inclusive of career entry, retention, and ongoing professional learning. The Tennessee LTSS story began with a WFD lens that led to intentional work to partner with the higher education system. The Illinois ECE story began with higher education faculty addressing pervasive challenges with career pathways and led to the use of a competency-based program as the point of alignment with the state's industry-recognized credentials and credential-related professional development system. In each of our stories, we began with questions about pathway challenges and the ways a competency-based program could help us resolve those challenges.

Appendix 1A

 YOUR TURN

Defining the pathway problem requires exploring disconnects and issues within and between educational and workplace context. Fill in the following table based on your own assessment of career pathway and workforce context challenges unique to your field. For each challenge identified, consider the present status of the challenge, your desired goal, and how you will collect data over time.

Reflect on your responses in the previous table.
Then, consider each of the following questions in Table 1.2:

- Are the issues/challenges identified specific to the field compared to the workforce in general?
- Are the issues/challenges defined by specific geography, time, or any other circumstantial factor?

TABLE 1.2
Career Pathway Challenges in Educational and Workplace Contexts

Career Pathway Challenges in the Educational Context			
What challenges exist with regard to recruiting and preparing professionals?			
Identified Challenge	*Present Status*	*Goal*	*Data Collection Strategies*

Career Pathway Challenges in the Workplace Context			
What challenges exist related to workforce participation, performance, and pathway progression/ persistence?			
Identified Challenge	*Present Status*	*Goal*	*Data Collection Strategies*

Based on your responses in the table and to the previous questions:

- What specific pathway problem(s) can be identified?
- What are the origins of identified pathway problems?
- What is the overall impact of identified pathway problems on students and the broader field?

References

Bernoteit, S. A., Darragh Ernst, J. C., & Latham, N. I. (2016). *Voices from the field: Collaborative innovations in early childhood educator preparation*. Illinois Education Research Council; Illinois Board of Higher Education.

Book, P. A. (2014). *All hands on deck: Ten lessons from early adopters of competency-based education*. Western Interstate Commission for Higher Education. http://files.eric.ed.gov/fulltext/ED546830.pdf

Burnette, D. M. (2016). The renewal of competency-based education: A review of the literature. *Journal of Continuing Higher Education*, *64*(2), 84–93. https://doi.org/10.1080/07377363.2016.1177704

Bushway, D., Dodge, L., & Long, C. (2018). *A leaders' guide to competency-based education: From inception to implementation*. Stylus.

Camacho, D. J., & Legare, J. M. (2016). Shifting gears in the classroom—movement toward personalized learning and competency-based education. *The Journal of Competency-Based Education*, *1*(4), 151–156. https://doi.org/10.1002/cbe2.1032

Darragh Ernst, J. C., Latham, N. I., & Bernoteit, S. A. (2016). Listening to voices from the field: Implications for higher education. In S. A. Bernoteit, J. C. Darragh Ernst, & N. I. Latham (Eds.), *Voices from the field: Collaborative innovations in early childhood educator preparation* (pp. 305–324). Illinois Education Research Council; Illinois Board of Higher Education.

Daugherty, L., Davis, V. L., & Miller, T. (2015). *Competency-based education programs in Texas: An innovative approach to higher education*. RAND Corporation. http://www.rand.org/pubs/research_reports/RR1239-1.html

Dodge, L., Bushway, D. J., & Long, C. S. (2018). *A leader's guide to competency-based education: From inception to implementation*. Stylus.

Ganzglass, E., Bird, K., & Prince, H. (2011). *Giving credit where credit is due: Creating a competency-based qualifications framework for postsecondary education and training*. Center for Law and Social Policy (CLASP). https://www.clasp.org/publications/report/brief/giving-credit-where-credit-due-creating-competency-based-qualifications

Garrett, R., & Lurie, H. (2016). *Deconstructing CBE: An assessment of institutional activity, goals, and challenges in higher education*. Lumina Foundation. https://www.luminafoundation.org/files/resources/deconstructing-cbe.pdf

Gomez, R. E., Kagan, S. L., & Fox, E. A. (2015). Professional development of the early childhood education teaching workforce in the United States: An overview. *Professional Development in Education*, *41*(2), 169–186. https://doi.org/10.1080/19415257.2014.986820

Haynes, E., Zeiser, K., Surr, W., Hauser, A., Clymer, L., Walston, J., Bitter, C., & Yang, R. (2016). *Looking under the hood of competency-based education: The relationship between competency-based education practices and students' learning skills, behaviors, and dispositions*. Nellie Mae Education Foundation. https://www.air.org/sites/default/files/downloads/report/CBE-Study%20Full%20Report.pdf

Illinois Network of Child Care Resource and Referral Agencies. (2014). *Facts about the early care and education workforce in Illinois*. Gateways to Opportunity Illinois Professional Development System.

Jenkins, D., & Fink, J. (2015). *What we know about transfer*. Columbia University, Teachers College, Community College Research Center.

Laitinen, A. (2012). *Cracking the credit hour*. New America Foundation. https://static.newamerica.org/attachments/2334-cracking-the-credit-hour/Cracking_the_Credit_Hour_Sept5_0.ab0048b12824428cba568ca359017ba9.pdf

Latorre, M., & Batchelor, M. (2016). Providing a pathway to degree completion for child care associates in rural southern Illinois. In S. A. Bernoteit, J. C. Darragh Ernst, & N. I. Latham (Eds.), *Voices from the field: Collaborative innovations in early childhood educator preparation* (pp. 66–81). Illinois Education Research Council; Illinois Board of Higher Education.

Lipscomb University. (n.d.). *Technical assistance report to Bureau of TennCare on the Quality Improvement in Long Term Services and Supports (QuILTSS) Initiative.* https://www.tn.gov/content/dam/tn/tenncare/documents/TennCareReport.pdf

Long, C. (2017, April 21). *Understanding competency-based education & the national landscape* [Paper presentation]. Gateways to Opportunity conference. Bloomington, IL, United States.

Lumina Foundation for Education. (2015). *Connecting credentials: Making the case for reforming the U.S. credentialing system.* https://www.luminafoundation.org/files/resources/making-the-case.pdf

Mathien, T., Nepstad, C., Potenza, A., Kim, J., & Mertes, W. (2016). Building on trust: How three institutions came together to create an innovative partnership for student transfer. In S. A. Bernoteit, J. C. Darragh Ernst, & N. I. Latham (Eds.), *Voices from the field: Collaborative innovations in early childhood educator preparation* (pp. 102–121). Illinois Education Research Council; Illinois Board of Higher Education.

McIntyre, C., Thompson, S. D., King, D., Smith, R., & Toliver, M. (2016). Career pathways in early childhood in rural communities. In S. A. Bernoteit, J. C. Darragh Ernst, & N. I. Latham (Eds.), *Voices from the field: Collaborative innovations in early childhood educator preparation* (pp. 224–237). Illinois Education Research Council; Illinois Board of Higher Education.

Monaghan, D. B., & Attewell, P. (2014). The community college route to the bachelor's degree. *Educational Evaluation and Policy Analysis.* Advance online publication. https://doi.org/10.3102/0162373714521865

Morel, N. J., & Griffiths, B. (2018). *Redefining competency-based education: Competence for life.* Business Expert Press.

President's Committee for People with Intellectual Disabilities. (2017). *Report to the president 2017: America's direct support workforce crisis: Effects on people with intellectual disabilities, families, communities and the U.S. economy.* https://acl.gov/sites/default/files/programs/2018-02/2017%20PCPID%20Full%20Report_0.PDF

Pruitt, R., Diez, C., Livesey, K., & Szymczak, M. (2016). Shifting the balance: Re-envisioning early childhood education preparation design through meaningful c ollaboration. In S. A. Bernoteit, J. C. Darragh Ernst, & N. I. Latham (Eds.), *Voices from the field: Collaborative innovations in early childhood educator preparation* (pp. 144–161). Illinois Education Research Council; Illinois Board of Higher Education.

Schilder, D. (2016). *Early childhood teacher education policies: Research review and state trends.* Center on Enhancing Early Learning Outcomes. http://ceelo.org/wpcontent/uploads/2016/04/ceelo_policy_report_ec_teach_education_policies_final_for_web_2016_04.pdf

Steinhaus, P., & Walker, D. (2016). Cross-institutional advising and curriculum agreements: Supports for transfer and degree completion in early childhood programs. In S. A. Bernoteit, J. C. Darragh Ernst, & N. I. Latham (Eds.), *Voices from the field: Collaborative innovations in early childhood educator preparation* (pp. 46–65). Illinois Education Research Council; Illinois Board of Higher Education.

Step 2

ESTABLISH THE COMPETENCY FRAMEWORK

Analysis of Professional Expectations That Define the Field

Central Question: How should the standards, regulations, and best practices that guide the field inform development of the competency framework?

Step 1 of our CDPM focuses on defining the career pathway challenges that a competency-based program will address based on careful exploration of relevant contexts. As noted, these pathway challenges can be identified through analysis of career preparation and performance challenges, including:

- low institutional retention rates
- a lack of student degree or credential completion
- excessive credit hour attainment in pursuit of a targeted degree or credential coupled with increased time and cost to completion (Jenkins & Fink, 2015; Monaghan & Attewell, 2014)
- the absence of graduates/completers obtaining or persisting in intended workforce roles
- a lack of graduate/completer demonstration of required knowledge and skills within the workplace
- graduate/completer difficulty progressing in career pathways based on education attainment (Bernoteit et al., 2016)

This chapter highlights Step 2 of the CDPM, providing an overview of processes needed to establish the competency framework. The framework design process begins with identifying the formal expectations for the field. Formal expectations consist of any and all benchmarks, standards, rules, or specified legal requirements that guide or mandate a field at federal, state, and local levels. Ideally, there is a strong bidirectional relationship between the guidelines or mandates included in educational and workforce contexts. In this relationship, educational programs infuse and embed required workforce performance indicators in a way that is meaningful, seamless, and reflective of the knowledge and skills needed to be successful. In many cases, the same guidelines or mandates might inform both professional preparation and workforce contexts; in others, these standards might mirror one another.

Once the formal context is established, attention can turn to identifying informal contexts. At this point, competency program designers need to outline factors that may indirectly influence professional preparation and workplace performance. These factors include the following:

- levels of employment
- best practices in the field that are essential, but not included in factors shaping the formal context
- varied pathways for both professional and workforce development
- how these pathways differ in terms of scope, sequence, content, delivery, and workforce expectations

"Levels" of employment can be thought of as progression both between and within roles, for example, moving from an entry-level to more advanced employment role or moving from novice to more experienced within a specific employment role. Best practices in the field that are not included in the formal context might include such things as an emerging knowledge base that has not yet been codified. Varied pathways for professional and workforce development can include, for example, noncredit bearing, credit bearing, microcredential and credential seeking, or degree seeking.

Understanding formal and informal contexts ensures that the competency framework designed is responsive to field-based and educational requirements, employment opportunities within the field, existing workforce pathways, and factors that are not codified in standards, yet are considered best practice. Careful attention to both formal and informal contexts will ensure framework flexibility, which in turn supports development across and within roles. Additionally, a flexible framework is resilient to changes in the external context, avoiding the need for revisions each time there is a shift in industry standards and expectations.

When working with multiple professional standard sets that inform preparation and performance, competency designers must establish the breadth of each standard set as well as how these sets intersect. This knowledge emerges from content analyses of all standards that influence preparation and workforce performance. In a deconstruction-reconstruction approach, this analysis lends insight into identifying which standard set is foundational—or the broadest and most inclusive—thereby encompassing all other standards. The following process can be used to determine which professional standard set is primary:

- Review each of the relevant formal and informal contexts.
- Look for commonalities across professional standard sets, guidelines, and accrediting requirements, as applicable. For example, are state and local standards derived from national standards? Are accrediting standards based on national guidelines?
- Identify the common denominator(s) among standard sets, guidelines, and accrediting requirements. If there is more than one, establish which is considered most foundational in the field, or most impactful across educational and workforce contexts.

This process is similar for competency development utilizing a framework origin approach, with the exception that, instead of being based on a standard set representing a common denominator, competency performance indicators are derived from and representative of a composite of industry standards.

Whether the approach used is one of deconstruction-reconstruction or framework origin, the primary standard set that is established or selected is responsive to both formal and informal contexts. For example, educational and workforce contexts in the field of nursing might include state and local standards that represent an adaptation of national standards. National standards, in this case, would be considered the primary standard set. The primary standard set serves as the content for the developing framework. The review and integration of all relevant contexts and standard sets leads to the development of performance expectations for an individual when demonstrating knowledge, skills, abilities, and intellectual behaviors across different levels of proficiency within workplace roles. In other words, integration of all contexts and standard sets allows for indicators to be written that illustrate what performance looks like when an individual is considered proficient at a respective workplace level or role in comparison to industry expectations.

Knowledge of the broader context also plays a key role when aligning the resulting primary content set. A well-aligned primary standard set adapts to contextual demands and is relevant across professional development and workforce contexts. Therefore, you do not need to change, alter, or explain the standard set content when considering levels of employment, engaging in discourse regarding best practices in the field, or aligning content with academic learning outcomes. The primary content set is aligned across workforce and professional preparation, and provides insight into scope, sequence, delivery, and workforce expectations. When the primary content set is well established and aligned in the informal context, the set is inherently meaningful to the profession regardless of the context.

 ## Remodeling the House: The Illinois ECE Story

As noted in Step 1, the Illinois ECE example represents a household remodel, where the bones of the structure were intact, and redesign was layered over those bones in response to pressing challenges. In the Illinois ECE example, competency performance indicators were developed based on well-established standards that existed within a highly regulated field. For the deconstruction-reconstruction process to be successful, the competency framework established needed to be inclusive of relevant factors in the broader context. This breadth of knowledge provided the broad foundation for the sorting of existing benchmarks/standards into contextually relevant themes/competency categories, resulting in the creation of a competency framework that is both meaningful and responsive. Together, these processes ensure professional preparation incorporates needed knowledge, skills, and intellectual behaviors for workforce entry, performance, and progression.

In the field of ECE in Illinois, formal and informal contexts were shaped by the variety of settings serving children ages birth through 8 years. These settings include community-based programs (such as family child care and child-care centers), state-funded programs (including Preschool for All and kindergarten through second grade in public schools), and federally funded programs (such as Head Start and Early Head Start). The formal standards associated with each of these settings vary, as do professional preparation requirements (including such things as the level of education needed to access and progress in a specific professional role).

Because the end goal of the Illinois framework was to unify and clarify as opposed to further confuse existing opportunities, careful accounting of varied standards, pathways, and requirements was needed. From this point, sorting into competency labels, inclusive of macro themes/competency categories, began.

Determining the primary content set within Illinois ECE required exploring commonalities among the varied formal professional preparation requirements for practitioners. As noted in Step 1, requirements varied based on role, place of employment, and the authorizing agency. Each of the standards impacting professional development is aligned with Gateways to Opportunity ECE Credentials. The Gateways ECE credentials are comprised of benchmarks that were originally developed with broad input from varied stakeholders in the early childhood field (including higher education faculty and practitioners within the workforce).

Table 2.1 provides an example of the relationship between Gateways benchmarks, Illinois Professional Teaching Standards, and NAEYC Standards for Professional Preparation. The first column of this example represents one of the Gateways ECE benchmarks. The other two columns represent the aligned Illinois Professional Teaching Standards and NAEYC Standards for Professional Preparation. The Gateways ECE benchmarks represent the primary content set, as these are as follows:

- inclusive of each of the other standard sets
- required in state teacher licensure
- used as the credential content within higher education programs
- required within the state's quality rating improvement system

Once the primary content set for the framework is established, the competency framework can emerge.

In the Illinois ECE deconstruction-construction approach, how competency performance indicators were sequenced and leveled was an essential aspect of framework development. In the Illinois model, *sequencing* refers

TABLE 2.1
Relationships Between Gateways ECE Benchmarks, Illinois Professional Teaching Standards, and NAEYC Standards for Professional Preparation

Gateways ECE Benchmarks	*Illinois Professional Teaching Standards*	*NAEYC Standards for Professional Preparation*
(Levels 2–4: A1) Articulates the relationship between theories of typical and atypical growth, development, and learning and early education practices, birth through age 8.	**2A:** Understands theories and philosophies of learning and human development as they relate to the range of students in the classroom.	**1a:** Knowing and understanding young children's characteristics and needs, from birth through age 8. **1b:** Knowing and understanding the multiple influences on early development and learning.

to the arrangement of competency performance indicators, and requires that foundational indicators are mastered prior to developing higher level capabilities. For example, a teacher must have a fundamental understanding of children's development and learning prior to being able to effectively plan lessons. *Leveling*, within the Illinois competency framework, reflects specific roles in the field and the accumulation of additional expertise and skill as individuals progress from entry-level staff to more advanced positions and beyond. When leveling is applied to a specific role, it is useful to consider what a novice practitioner might know and be able to do as compared to an experienced or more educated practitioner in that same role. Regardless of how competency performance indicators are sequenced, it is essential that these indicators reflect the expectations of the workforce context (Bernoteit et al., 2016).

In Illinois, leveling and sequencing were critical components of the framework established. As presented in Step 1, Illinois utilized a career pathway model that delineated performance expectations for leveled workforce roles in the field of ECE. The working framework necessitated that the knowledge, skills, and intellectual behaviors needed for successful performance at the entry-level/foundational role (teaching assistant) were developed, refined, and expanded with additional learning and expertise needed for the subsequent ECE roles of teacher, lead teacher, and master teacher. The standards selected as the primary set needed to be clustered to align with these roles and related expectations for performance. This clustering included:

- creating a *meaningful sequence*, representing how required proficiencies are related in terms of scaffolding (e.g., what knowledge, skills, and intellectual behaviors are foundational to the development of additional expertise, and how this expertise is supported in meaningful ways)
- *logical leveling*, defining roles where knowledge and skills are considered essential (e.g., required for job performance)

Leveling can also apply to the composition of each individual credential within a stacked pathway. As previously noted, competency frameworks can be based on an infrastructure that communicates the accumulation of knowledge and skills within a particular role (e.g., how an individual progresses from novice to expert in that role). Frameworks can also encapsulate progression within a field (e.g., how an individual progresses from entry-level to leadership roles).

The reconstruction process required reorganizing the 347 benchmarks that comprised the original Gateways ECE credentials into specific, measurable, observable competency performance indicators reflective of the knowledge, skills, and intellectual behaviors required for particular employment roles (Assistant Teacher-Level 2, Teacher-Level 3, Lead Teacher-Level 4, and Master Teacher-Level 5). For the primary content set of the ECE benchmarks, two specific criteria were used for examining, sorting, and grouping.

The first criterion was to determine what knowledge or skill is considered foundational for the developmental progression of a professional. For example, prior to applying the skill of collaborating with families, professionals must have knowledge of appropriate communication strategies and the ability to apply these strategies. Knowledge of appropriate communication strategies, therefore, is the foundation to application of communication and collaboration skills. The second criterion included determining what knowledge or skill is considered essential within a professional role. A Gateways Credential Level 3 teacher in an early childhood classroom is responsible for planning and implementing activities and interactions supportive of a young child's healthy development and well-being. An assistant teacher would not be expected to have knowledge and skills supportive of curriculum planning and implementation but would be expected to interact with children in a manner supportive of healthy development and well-being. Knowledge of appropriate interactions and the skills to engage in those interactions, in this example, represent foundational knowledge and skills for each professional working with young children. Planning and implementing activities that enhance children's development in those areas represents a higher level knowledge and skill, and therefore is required for the role of the Gateways Credential Level 3 teacher. This progression is reflective of the Lumina Foundation's Degree Qualifications Profile, focusing on describing what students should know and be able to do as they progress through credential attainment (Lumina Foundation, 2014).

This leveling and sequencing process was conducted by a core group of early childhood faculty who reviewed each of the 347 benchmarks and—through a process of consensus—established at which level each individual benchmark was essential for the practitioner to know or be able to demonstrate. The established framework provided grouping categories (from teacher assistant through teacher leader); if a knowledge or skill was considered absolutely essential for any practitioner working in an early childhood classroom, it was placed at the role of the assistant teacher. As the framework was leveled and tied to stackable credentials, each level that built on Level 2 would include the requirements of each preceding role. The categorization of benchmarks was further informed by the sorting team's knowledge of role expectations and the developmental progression of practitioner knowledge, skills, and intellectual behaviors. It is important to note that this process must be repeated based on the number of subset criteria.

As we sorted our benchmarks, we asked ourselves if the benchmark represented essential knowledge, skills, and intellectual behaviors required for success for the following:

- all practitioners working with young children and their families?
- those who are responsible for classroom development, implementation, and assessment?
- those who are responsible for leading others in classroom development, implementation, and assessment?

This aspect of the process both informed and was informed by roles in the field. Additionally, this part of the process provided further exploration of how benchmarks were intricately related, serving to ensure that knowledge of a skill will precede application, and application will precede the capacity to develop that knowledge and skill in others. In many ways, this aspect of our sorting process provided an additional checkpoint and lens of accuracy, with the assumption that higher levels would be inclusive of benchmarks related to leading, and lower levels inclusive of benchmarks related to knowledge.

Content analysis was the final step in developing the competency framework. In this step, the previously established primary analysis criteria becomes the focal lens through which to sort the identified primary set. It is important to note that there may be more than one lens, meaning that this sorting process can happen multiple times. The broader context (the workforce, education systems, etc.) determines which criteria are meaningful in terms of the sorting process. As noted, this can include such factors as workplace roles, professional themes, a continuum from knowing to leading, or depth of content from simple to complex.

 Building From a Blueprint: The Tennessee LTSS Story

The field of LTSS in the state of Tennessee spans multiple settings and populations served. In turn, TQI workforce development programs are specifically built to cut across multiple settings that serve adults with disabilities as well as the aging population. These settings include home- and community-based settings, assisted living facilities, nursing facilities, and memory care programs. Because the term "direct service worker" refers to any individual in the field of LTSS who supports adults with disabilities or the aging population, job roles can vary greatly, and the pathway to attaining those roles differs depending on expectations of those roles. Figure 2.1 illustrates the various frameworks for TQI's competency-based workforce development program.

To establish the informal and formal contexts relative to the field of LTSS, TQI focused on the alignment of stakeholder needs to the adoption of the Final Competency Set for the Direct Service Workforce implemented through the National Direct Service Workforce Resource Center (DSW RC). The Final Competency Set implemented through DSW RC is the product of a multiphase research project—Road Map of Core Competencies for the Direct Service Workforce, funded by the Centers for Medicare & Medicaid Services (CMS)—to identify a common set of core competencies across community-based LTSS sectors. The purpose of the research project was to assist with a standardized approach to training and education of the DSW. The intent of the Final Competency Set is twofold: (a) provide a standardized approach to education and training, and (b) serve as a foundation for career lattices.

The CMS Final Competency Set, consisting of 12 core competency areas for the DSW, was released in 2014. These competency areas

Figure 2.1. Framework origin for the QuILTSS Institute's CBE Certificate in Long-Term Services and Supports (LTSS) program.

included communication; person-centered practices; professionalism and ethics; evaluation and observation; community inclusion and networking; community living skills and supports; health and wellness; empowerment and advocacy; cultural competency; safety; crisis prevention and intervention; and education, training, and self-development. Figure 2.2 shows an example of an adopted competency area. The CMS Final Competency Set directly ties to the State of Tennessee's value-based purchasing program, in which staff training is a significant quality measure resulting in higher rates of Medicaid reimbursement for the provider agency, and ultimately for the individual staff members who successfully complete workforce development (WFD) training through TQI.

From this foundation, the performance indicators could be leveled and sequenced. In the Tennessee model, sequencing reflected courses that led to the attainment of microcredentials. These microcredentials were tied to incentive payments. Note that each individual competency development process may have additional criteria that are relevant for examining, sorting, and grouping.

Leveling and sequencing became important as work with the TBR continued to unfold, and the Bureau of TennCare began aligning incentive payments to staff training. TQI organized the 12 WFD competencies into 12 corresponding competency courses. Once a learner successfully demonstrates proficiency in the 12 WFD competency courses, the 12 microcredentials representative of each course weave together into the full QuILTSS WFD credential. Meanwhile, the TBR worked with TQI to determine how a learner is likely to progress most successfully through the 12 courses to

Figure 2.2. CMS Direct Service Workforce Core Competency: Communication.

---

1. Competency Area: Communication (3)

The DSW builds trust and productive relationships with people s/he supports, coworkers, and others through respectful and clear verbal and written communication.

Skill Statements
The direct service worker:

    a. Uses positive and respectful verbal, nonverbal, and written communication a way that can be understood by the individual, and actively listens and responds to him or her in a respectful, caring manner.
    b. Explains services and service terms to the individual being supported and his or her family members.
    c. Communicates with the individual and his or her family in a respectful and culturally appropriate way.

From the Centers for Medicare & Medicaid *Final Competency Set*, 2014.

earn the full QuILTSS WFD credential, which translates to a postsecondary certificate in LTSS. It is important to note that aligning the pay incentives to learner progress was the ultimate goal in order to motivate satisfactory academic progress through the courses in pursuit of successful completion of the 18-credit-hour postsecondary certificate in LTSS. In order to successfully group courses into semester-based bundles, subject matter experts (SMEs) and TennCare provided recommendations for appropriate course sequencing relative to workforce needs. For example, SMEs considered questions such as:

- What competency areas are foundational to learner success?
- In what ways should the competencies build on each other to lead the learner to successful performance in the workplace?
- How should a learner progress through the competency courses once bundles are identified? Should learners work through courses simultaneously within each four-course bundle, or should learners work through courses one at a time within each four-course bundle?
- How will successful completion of each four-course bundle translate to pay incentives?
- How will successful completion of each four-course bundle translate to college-level credit?
- How will satisfactory academic progress be met with the four-course bundles?

As a result, course bundles were grouped in the following manner to weave into the full QuILTSS credential (see Table 2.2).

TABLE 2.2
Course Bundles

Bundle 1	Bundle 2	Bundle 3
Communication Person-Centered Practices Evaluation and Observation Professionalism and Ethics	Community Inclusion and Networking Community Living Skills and Supports Health and Wellness Empowerment and Advocacy	Cultural Competency Safety Crisis Prevention and Intervention Education, Training, and Self-Development

These three distinct bundles were created in collaboration with essential partners. TQI leveled and sequenced the 12 competency areas and respective courses with the goal of creating clear educational and career pathways in LTSS. Clear educational pathways allow a TBR student to complete one bundle per semester, leading to the postsecondary certificate in LTSS—18 hours of college-level credit that can be embedded in a variety of associate degree programs, in turn, embedding into bachelor's degree programs, and so forth. Additionally, the bundled structure allows for Tennessee students to access state lottery funds through programs including Tennessee Promise and Tennessee Reconnect. As noted previously, in 2013, then-Governor Bill Haslam launched the Drive to 55 to increase the number of Tennesseans with a postsecondary degree or certificate to 55% by 2025. As a result, the Haslam administration and General Assembly established both the Tennessee Promise, which allows high school graduates meeting certain requirements to attend 2 years of community or technical college free of tuition and fees, and the Tennessee Reconnect scholarship, which provides free technical college for adults. Similarly, clear career pathways allow staff to earn a pay increase with each four-course bundle they successfully complete through required demonstration of those competency areas. With each four-course bundle successfully completed, the staff moves through the career pathway as a Community Specialist I, Community Specialist II, and Community Specialist III, respectively. The learner may choose to work their way up the career ladder or grow in their current role; regardless, their increased competence is recognized. In the Tennessee LTSS story, adoption of the primary competency set with clear career and educational pathways sets the stage for defining robust and meaningful competency statements relevant in higher education as well as in the LTSS workforce.

Points of Intersection: Illinois and Tennessee

Fully accounting for formal and informal contexts in both Illinois and Tennessee required a clear understanding of educational pathways, roles, funding streams, and all required standards impacting differing areas of the field. In the case of Illinois, this step ensured that the primary content set that was identified, selected, and developed was flexible, was inclusive of varied professional development and workforce expectations, and addressed existing challenges. In the case of Tennessee, this step was critical in ensuring that the competencies developed were inclusive of federal, state, and industry standards as well as subject matter expertise.

The primary content set established for both Illinois and Tennessee encompassed industry and professional development requirements. The Tennessee primary content set emerged in the workforce and then was mapped into professional development requirements, while the Illinois primary content set emerged in higher education and was reflective of industry standards. These differing points of origin influence how the primary content sets were developed and aligned within professional development and the workplace.

The Illinois and Tennessee models, due to the differences noted in competency development origins, varied in their conceptualization of leveling and sequencing. In Illinois, leveling and sequencing applied to competency progression within higher education credentials that were aligned to varied roles in the field. In Tennessee, leveling and sequencing applied to roles in the field, and competencies represented progression within those roles (e.g., novice to expert within one role). The variance in approach that each model took influenced how the primary content set was sorted and arranged.

Appendix 2A

 YOUR TURN

At this point, you have considered the breadth of factors needed to develop the competency frameworks and explored foundational steps involved in framework development. Consider the following relative to framework development for your targeted field:

Identify commonalities across professional standard sets, guidelines, and accrediting requirements. Be sure to consider such questions as:

Do state and local standards align with national standards (if applicable)?

Are accrediting standards based on national guidelines?
Identify the common denominator(s) among standard sets, guidelines, and accrediting requirements.

If there is more than one, establish which is most foundational in the field or most impactful across educational and workforce contexts.

Select the one that is most impactful as your primary set.

References

Bernoteit, S. A., Darragh Ernst, J. C., & Latham, N. I. (2016). *Voices from the field: Collaborative innovations in early childhood educator preparation.* Illinois Education Research Council; Illinois Board of Higher Education.

Centers for Medicare & Medicaid. (2014). *Final competency set.* http://mykapp.org/wp-content/uploads/2016/10/CMS-dsw-core-competencies-final-set-2014.pdf

Jenkins, D., & Fink, J. (2015). *What we know about transfer.* Columbia University, Teachers College, Community College Research Center.

Lumina Foundation. (2014). *The degree qualifications profile: A learning-centered framework for what college graduates should know and be able to do to earn the associate, bachelor's, or master's degree.* https://www.luminafoundation.org/files/resources/dqp.pdf

Monaghan, D. B., & Attewell, P. (2014). The community college route to the bachelor's degree. *Educational Evaluation and Policy Analysis.* Advance online publication. https://doi.org/10.3102/0162373714521865

Step 3

DRAFT COMPETENCY STATEMENTS

Central Question: Based on the analysis in Step 2, what knowledge, skills, and intellectual behaviors are necessary for successful performance in the workplace role?

This chapter outlines Step 3 in the CDPM: drafting meaningful competency statements. The product of Step 3 is the first draft of robust performance indicators to clearly communicate what current and future practitioners are expected to know and do. Step 3 is grounded in a deep analysis of the knowledge, skills, and intellectual behaviors that will be defined by the performance indicators, and it reflects the backward design process, which relies on building the program with the end in mind. Step 3 closely relates to the first stage of backward design, where competencies are identified and defined. This ensures the outcomes you want the learner to have at the end of the learning experience are clearly stated and defined, answering the question "What do you want the learner to know and be able to do?"

The performance indicators developed in Step 3 should state in robust, clear language the knowledge, skills, and intellectual behaviors needed in a way that is observable, measurable, and able to be captured. The correct capture of these indicators sets the foundation for use of the competencies throughout preparation for employment, professional development, and performance evaluation in the workplace. It is important to note that although Step 3 serves as a draft of your performance indicators, the process of competency development is far from complete. You will note, and we will continue to reiterate, how important each remaining step is in the polishing and honing of your draft performance indicators to make them sustainable and usable in the field.

Three questions guide the creation of initial competency performance indicators:

1. How can we *draft indicator statements* that describe what performance looks like for each competency area identified through the content analysis in Step 2?
2. How do our drafted performance indicators "fit" into and *reflect the competency area*?
3. What vetting process can be used to get *industry/field constituent feedback* on the draft performance indicators?

We will use our two examples from the fields of ECE and LTSS to explore each of these questions. As we dig into our two examples for this step, remember these examples demonstrate two different approaches to the CDPM. Our Illinois ECE example reflects a "deconstruction-reconstruction" approach, whereas our Tennessee LTSS example demonstrates a "framework origin" approach. As we have discussed in earlier chapters, these two approaches really equate to either a substantive "remodel" of the structure (deconstruction-reconstruction) as in our ECE example, or "building a structure based on a blueprint," as in the case of our LTSS example.

 Remodeling the House: The Illinois ECE Story

At this point, our industry benchmarks and expectations had been through several levels of content analysis and sorting (Step 2). This process resulted in groupings or "buckets" of professional benchmarks. It was important, as we examined each bucket through our professional lens and knowledge of the field, to refer to the alignment of *all* industry standards and expectations that was also done as part of Step 2. This allowed us to revise the bucket as needed, ensuring it captured all it represented and cleaning it for any redundancy.

It was also meaningful as we drafted our performance indicators to consider each one individually and ensure its stand-alone value and depth. These indicators needed to be substantive enough to stand alone without the support or context of other performance indicators while working together to seamlessly support and reflect the competency area. In the ECE example, we were mandated to preserve the original benchmark language, which limited flexibility in cluster wording. You may find the same kind of constraints in testing, federal and state licensure rules, and other mandates. From the required benchmarks, we created draft statements that were concise, measurable, and represented the knowledge, skills, and/or intellectual behaviors in the bucket.

Drafting Representative Performance Indicators

In the Illinois ECE work, the content analysis described in Step 2 provided "tight" professional expectation buckets, which served as the foundation for a performance indicator. The following is an example of a bucket of benchmarks that emerged for the teacher assistant level in the competency area of Human Growth and Development (HGD):

- articulates the relationship between theories of typical and atypical growth, development, and learning and early education practices, birth through age 8
- charts the milestones that indicate various stages in all developmental domains
- gives examples of ways individual differences in ability, attitudes, interests, and values impact children's growth and development
- identifies the characteristics associated with developmental delays, developmental disabilities, and risk factors that influence growth and development
- identifies the unique patterns which distinguish typical from atypical development
- describes the unique developmental and learning needs of children in different age groups and with diverse abilities

From the previous benchmark bucket, the following draft performance indicator was authored:

- *HGD1: Identifies and describes theories of typical and atypical growth in all developmental domains as well as the interaction between individual and contextual factors on development and learning*

It is wise to also think about, at this point, how you might begin to organize or number your performance indicators in a way that identifies competency area and level, reflecting the competency framework established in Step 1. For example, the previous ECE performance indicator, HGD1, uses the organizer/citation to communicate the competency area (Human Growth and Development). It further communicates the performance level (1), which specifies a foundational performance indicator in the Human Growth and Development competency area.

To further extend this example, HGD5 provides an illustration of a drafted performance indicator statement in the same competency area (HGD: Human Growth and Development). In this draft performance indicator, the skill communicated is considered essential for Master Teachers (Level 5), and was informed by the following benchmarks:

- identifies relevant developmental research and child development data to inform evidence-based practice
- makes decisions about evidence-based practices supporting children's learning and development
- incorporates research, developmental theories, and observational data in decisions

The resulting higher level performance indicator from this bucket was:

- *HGD5: Integrates research, developmental theories, and observational data to make decisions about evidence-based practice supporting children's learning and development*

This example further communicates sequencing within the established framework and how HGD1 is essential to successful demonstration of HGD5. Identifying and describing development (HGD1) is the first step in an ECE teacher's ability to integrate research, theory, and data (HGD5).

Assessing Competency Framework "Fit"

At this point it was essential to do a preliminary review of the draft performance indicators to assess that they were representative of the content analysis from Step 2. This review included attempting to "fit" the draft performance indicators into the competency area framework previously established as part of the content analysis. We asked ourselves the question "Do our performance indicators individually and collectively represent the integrity of the buckets and coding that emerged from Step 2?"

For our ECE preliminary review we examined our performance indicators against our established criteria. For our review this included examining the following:

- how the draft performance indicator accurately represented the competency framework area it was aligned with
- how the draft performance indicator accurately represented best practice
- how the draft performance indicator represented leveling within actual professional application or levels of position (if applicable)

Table 3.1 articulates the performance indicators for the Human Growth and Development area. As you can see, this preliminary review resulted in leveled (simple to complex), content-rich, measurable statements.

Each question in our model was an opportunity to refine, polish, and sharpen the draft performance indicators. An important next step in this "polishing" was creating a process for expert review of the performance indicators moving forward.

Statement Vetting: Constituent Feedback

Because our ECE example utilized a deconstruction-reconstruction approach, the role of constituent/expert review in Step 3 of our CDPM ensured that each drafted performance indicator accurately represented the existing standards and benchmarks we were accountable to while expressing observable, measurable best practices in the field. The process of determining the validity of each performance indicator required several feedback loops. At each stage of the review process, changes were made to indicator language, framework sequencing, and in some cases, indicator bucketing. The outcomes of this review process—and related revisions—were stronger, substantive, representative performance indicators.

This vetting and review process involved identifying stakeholder groups of experts and professionals who vetted indicators and provided feedback for statement revision. These groups were essential not only for this step but also for review and vetting in all subsequent steps. Groups were established to represent the workforce and career pathway challenges identified in Step 1.

In organizing and inviting the expert groups that would inform our Illinois ECE work, we sought several specific categories of representation. First, we identified constituents who would use the indicators to measure professional preparation and professional competence. These experts included faculty at both 2- and 4-year early childhood teacher preparation programs, as well as early childhood center directors and school administrators who would hire, evaluate, and make professional development decisions regarding professionals in the field.

Second, we identified constituents who were linked to the indicators organizationally. These experts included early childhood regulatory and credentialing agencies with responsibility for early childhood program and preparation program oversight and support. Lastly, we made sure our expert vetting teams included professionals who would actually use the performance indicators in planning professional development of in-service teachers, as well as practitioners at all levels who would be evaluated using the indicators.

TABLE 3.1
Gateways ECE Human Growth and Development Assessment

Assistant Teacher (Level 2)	Entry-Level Teacher (Level 3)	Teacher (Level 4-Associate Degree)	Lead Teacher (Level 5-Bachelor's Degree)
Human Growth and Development			
HGD1: Identifies and describes theories of typical and atypical growth in all developmental domains and the interaction between individual and contextual factors on development and learning.		HGD4: Interprets children's unique developmental patterns and identifies supportive resources for children who may require further assessment. Demonstrates knowledge of processes of first and second language acquisition.	HGD5: Integrates research, developmental theories, and observational data to make decisions about evidence-based practice supporting children's learning and development.
HGD2: Describes the interrelationship between developmental domains, holistic well-being, and adaptive/living skills.			
HGD3: Defines how cultural, familial, biological, and environmental influences, including stress, trauma, protective factors, and resilience, impact children's wellbeing and learning.			HGD6: Justifies and promotes the use of evidence-based practices supportive of each child's unique patterns of development and learning.

From Gateways to Opportunity, *ECE Toolbox*, n.d.

After expert groups were established, it was important to set up specific systems and timelines for review and feedback collection and analysis. Our expert groups were established statewide with the goal of wide representation. We employed specific technology tools to disseminate work for review, at times to the whole group and at other times to subgroups with expertise in a specific content area. Substantive feedback was also collected through face-to-face statewide meetings. Experts in standards review, alignment, and use were charged with collecting, analyzing, and summarizing feedback so it could be used to inform performance indicator revision.

 Building From a Blueprint: The Tennessee LTSS Story

A competency set was released to the field of LTSS in 2014 by CMS. This set consisted of 12 core competencies for the DSW. Because we were using a framework origin design, in alignment with Stage 1 of the backward design process, leveling and sequencing were an important component of the competency framework. As such, establishing levels of mastery across each competency area was a process of more narrowly defining expectations of what a learner should know and be able to do when they are considered "proficient" at identified levels of performance. The QuILTSS workforce development framework defined expectations for four levels of mastery, including Level 1—not yet proficient; Level 2—frontline DSW; Level 3—supervisor; and Level 4—agency owner/chief executive officer.

Drafting Representative Performance Indicators

In this framework origin competency-based program build, it was necessary to work with SMEs to identify and describe what performance looked like at each of the levels of mastery. In this program, levels of mastery were articulated for each of the 12 competency areas. Over 200 individuals volunteered and were organized into small core curriculum committees (CCCs) comprised of state-level stakeholders in the field such as LTSS providers as well as managed care organization representatives. Each CCC held monthly meetings and completed guided activities to create initial drafts of materials such as development guides and levels of mastery for their assigned competency area. The result of this build was 12 competency areas leveled by job role with behavioral descriptors that served as measurable performance indicators. These drafts were moved forward for further field vetting, review, feedback, and revision.

Assessing Competency Framework "Fit"

For our preliminary LTSS review and the multiple layers of review and feedback moving forward, the levels of mastery were examined for scope and sequence. Reviewing the scope of performance indicators was critical. Appropriate scope ensures the description of performance is expansive enough to encompass a range of observable behavioral examples indicative of the target competency area, and narrow enough to accurately and reliably observe and measure it. While scope is important to measurability, sequence is important to identifying what behavior looks like across levels of mastery, whether that be growth in a consistent job role, level of academic program, or employment pipeline. Ask yourself a key question when evaluating your competency area definitions: "Does the competency area definition, including the performance indicators, represent successful performance of that respective competency area at the identified level of mastery in the workplace, job role, or academic level?" As an example, Table 3.2 serves as a snapshot of levels of mastery for the Person-Centered Practices competency area (please note that this example is an excerpt and not the full Levels of Mastery tool).

Statement Vetting: Constituent Feedback

Levels of mastery created by the CCCs went through several layers of review and feedback vetting to secure competency area and performance indicator relevance to the field of LTSS. This process included the following:

1. A Stakeholder Advisory Group was created by identifying a select group of state leaders from the 12 CCCs who represented the different service delivery settings along with various geographic locations in Tennessee. The Stakeholder Advisory Group was asked to review and provide substantive feedback on competency area definitions and levels of mastery for the 12 competency areas based on their expertise and experiences in the field.
2. The leadership team from TennCare Long-Term Services and Supports provided review and feedback, including the collapse of the levels of mastery from five originally defined levels to four levels.
3. A leading SME specific to the nursing facility setting provided review and feedback for the 12 competency areas.
4. A national SME, considered the forward-thinking leader in the field of LTSS, was identified for each individual competency area to provide review and feedback.

TABLE 3.2
LTSS Levels of Mastery—Person-Centered Practices

1-Not Yet Proficient	2-DSW	3-Supervisor	4-Executive Manager
• Interacts with inappropriate cues such as eye-rolling or flat affect. • Rarely demonstrates nonverbal active listening behaviors such as leaning forward, head nodding, or eye contact. • May acknowledge speaker cues, however, does not adapt behavior to such cues (e.g., person nonverbally expresses resistance for bath and DSW moves forward with task without responding). • Rarely responds to individual preferences (e.g., cultural considerations) and does not adapt behavior based on such preferences (e.g., eye contact). • Often shows distraction during interactions but directs attention when prompted to do so.	• Gives full attention to person and task at hand. • Responds to speaker cues and adapts behavior based on cues in a variety of situations (e.g., DSW responds nonverbally to reassure the person of task such as eye contact and gentle touch). • Consistently interacts with positive facial expressions and body language (e.g., eye contact on eye level, smiles). • Responds to individual preferences (e.g., cultural considerations) of the speaker. • Keeps distractions to a minimum (e.g., cell phone use, shuffling papers).	• Proactively predicts how the person will respond and adjusts approach accordingly. • Responds to speaker cues and adapts behavior based on cues (e.g., across environments of support, cultural contexts, and individual preferences). • Consistently presents self as approachable by interacting with positive facial expressions and body language (e.g., eye contact on eye level, smiles). • Rarely shows distracted behaviors except in an emergency situation.	• Consistently demonstrates an approachable and responsive demeanor toward a variety of situations. • Shows awareness of situations around them and able to multitask to ensure intervention when needed (e.g., gestures a person's needs to another DSW while reading a progress report and acknowledging a family member's presence). • Establishes a physical presence by leading in daily activities. • Consistently uses sound diction when speaking with a collaborative tone of voice and clarity of speech. • Disagrees in a neutral, nonconfrontational manner when the situation arises.

Following this feedback, the full competency program was piloted, and feedback was sought specific to each of the 12 competency areas for comprehensiveness, gaps, relevance, and validity to the field of LTSS.

Points of Intersection: Illinois and Tennessee

Step 3 in this process captures the industry and professional standards and expectations and populates or fills the competency framework identified in Step 2 with substantive, rich indicators of performance that undergird the framework with their observable, measurable nature. Although the approaches vary, the fundamental outcome should be the same. Whether you find yourself in a situation where you are building the professional expectations "from the blueprint" or "remodeling" competency areas using legislated or systematically established standards or benchmarks, the creation of measurable, substantive indicators of performance remains the same. These indicators will serve as the foundation from which the competency areas can actually be used in the design of professional preparation programs and the evaluation of learners completing those programs. These performance indicators should also be able to be used in the structuring, design, and offering of professional development for the practitioner in the workforce and serve as a measurable plumb line for evaluating professional practice in the field.

Appendix 3A

 YOUR TURN

Drafting performance indicators requires attention to each of the processes outlined in the following tables. Using your framework developed in Step 2 of the competency development process model, prepare your own performance indicators by reproducing and completing the following table for each identified competency area.

Duplicate the following table for each competency area in your competency framework.

1. Take each cluster of standards from your content analysis and list each standard/benchmark in the cluster in column 1.
2. Next, in column 2 of the table, enter the alignment (if any) of all secondary professional standards/guidelines to the original primary standards cluster that align with the cluster but are not represented in the primary set.

3. Draft performance indicators that capture this cluster; this sounds simple but takes a while to craft, and as you will see going forward, it will continue to be edited and honed (columns 3 and 4).
4. Review each draft performance indicator and see if it best fits, out of all of the competency areas in your framework, in the area in which you have placed it. After all indicators are drafted in the competency area, make sure they are in sequential order from basic or simple to more complex competencies (column 5).
5. In column 6 provide a summary of the feedback you receive of these draft indicators when you do the initial vetting with stakeholder groups described.

TABLE 3.3
Competency Area Table

Competency Area						
#1 List each identified professional standard/ benchmark in this cluster.	#2 List alignment to other industry standards.	#3 Draft performance indicators	#4 Does it fully represent the competency area?	#5 Are performance indicators as a whole representative of expected performance of the competency?	#6 Provide feedback/ review comments.	List revisions made.

DRAFT COMPETENCY STATEMENTS

Competency Area						
#1 List each identified professional standard/ benchmark in this cluster.	#2 List alignment to other industry standards.	#3 Draft performance indicators	#4 Does it fully represent the competency area?	#5 Are performance indicators as a whole representative of expected performance of the competency?	#6 Provide feedback/ review comments.	List revisions made.

Duplicate and use the following table to help you organize stakeholders by expertise and the constituencies they represent.

TABLE 3.4
Stakeholders

	Name	Role/Group Representing	Expertise	Contact Information
Stakeholders who will use these competencies in developing workforce preparation programs and content				

Reference

Gateways to Opportunity. (n.d.). *ECE toolbox*. https://www.ilgateways.com/professional-development/higher-education-programs/ece-toolbox

Step 4

ESTABLISH COMPETENCY MEASURABILITY

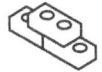 *Central Question: How will you know competence when you see it?*

In Step 3, draft performance indicators were developed. These draft indicators, which had not yet been scrutinized through the lens of measurability, were informed by knowledge, skills, and intellectual behaviors required within educational and workplace contexts (see Step 2).

In our CDPM, the next critical stage in the development of the performance indicators is determining the extent to which the draft performance indicators can be measured. Step 4 is fundamental to the eventual use of the performance indicators in developing, guiding, and evaluating professional practice. This step also serves to further refine, sequence, and contextualize the draft performance indicators. If a performance indicator is not measurable—if you cannot describe how you will know it when you see a professional doing it—it is useless.

Determining the measurability of the performance indicator creates a solid, quantifiable foundation for evaluating performance. This foundation not only refines the original indicators but also provides the assessment and evaluation foundation for CBE/CBL programs. Determining measurability involves the following:

- analyzing the performance indicator verb for measurability
- developing performance description statements that capture what the indicator looks like in action
- developing scoring tools that reflect ranges of indicator performance
- reviewing the proposed scoring tools for how well they assess the targeted indicator

This chapter will explain these elements of determining measurability, describe how both our Illinois and Tennessee stories tackled measurability, and give you an opportunity to think about measurability in your context. Just remember, although our focus in this step is developing indicator scoring tools, ensuring that the indicators are indeed measurable reflects either their strength or the need to return to the draft indicator and strengthen it to be more meaningful and measurable.

Analyzing Indicator Verbs for Measurability

To ensure measurability, it is important to specifically analyze the verbs chosen for each draft indicator. The work of determining and developing indicators may sometimes inhibit users from seeing the actual measurability of the verbs chosen, specifically when they are shrouded in the content language of a complete performance indicator statement. Therefore, examining each verb in an indicator by simply describing the resulting performance allows one to quickly see whether it is measurable. Verbs such as "understand," "know," "remember," "appreciate," and "consider" are all examples of verbs that can be difficult to measure.

It is critical to avoid making the mistake of defining indicators in a way that leads to common problems with measurement, including subjective evaluation. Subjective evaluations typically include performance described by inference, such as feelings and emotions, as well as covert behaviors, such as "understanding" or "knowing." The verbs you use to describe behavior become critically important in creating an objective, behaviorally based definition.

When examining indicator verbs, it is important to ask measurability questions such as the following:

- What does "understanding" look like?
- What will it look like if a practitioner "knows"?
- How will the professional demonstrate "remembering"?
- How is "appreciation" described?
- What level of "consideration" is enough?

As you can see, these questions highlight difficulty in verb measurability. It is obvious in these examples that performance is difficult to describe and subjective to measure, rendering the indicator useless.

Building Performance Criteria

The development of specific statements that describe the indicator in action involves crafting a descriptive "how you will know it when you see it" statement for each indicator. The performance criteria should specifically state what it will look like if a practitioner is demonstrating that performance at a specified level of performance. It should not be the restatement of the indicator but rather a substantive description of how you will know it when you see it in practice.

The behavioral sciences are a helpful resource in CBE. Behavioral science emphasizes the importance of operationally defining behavior in a way that is overt. Overt behavior is observable, and observable behavior is measurable (Cooper et al., 2019). The occurrence of behavior is readily apparent to the observer if defined in observable terms (Nock & Kurtz, 2005). To create effective performance criteria, it is important to describe behavior in observable and measurable terms that are clear, concise, and complete. Be mindful that the purpose of the definition is to describe the form of behavior expected in order to accurately measure it, and that directly relates to the verb you choose to describe the behavior and the expectation of performance from the learner.

Developing Performance Scoring Tools That Reflect Ranges of Indicator Performance

As we have discussed, performance indicators may employ higher level or lower level verbs at their core. Some competency areas may have indicators that reflect a mix of both, and therefore measurability tools differ. With lower level verbs (e.g., list, name, define, etc.), providing a "range of performance" would not be as helpful in measuring competency as specifically identifying, at a minimum, exactly what the competent professional should name, list, define, and so forth. In these cases, a scoring tool that utilizes binary, targeted criteria as opposed to leveled performance criteria might be a better scoring tool.

Performance indicators that employ a higher level verb are best evaluated with a scoring tool that describes "levels" of performance. This is developed using the indicator's performance criteria as the baseline performance expectation and developing the levels of performance stemming from there. This type of scoring tool is often created in a rubric format. Either way, once performance is defined or described, a tool to measure and assess competency should be developed using that performance criteria as the anchor.

Performance Criteria and Scoring Tool Review

Lastly, using the established stakeholder/review groups from Step 3, it is important to collect feedback on both how performance criteria are communicating what the performance indicator will look like in professional practice as well as how the drafted scoring tools measure the performance indicator. This is a complex review process and may be best assigned to specific groups of experts in each competency area. It is essential in this review to analyze and incorporate the feedback received. All feedback and revision needs to be considered, not just for the scoring tools, but also for the continued refining of performance criteria language and the draft performance indicator.

 ## Remodeling the House: The Illinois ECE Story

In our early childhood example, the analysis of our indicator verbs and creation of our performance criteria forced us to go back and reexamine some of our initial indicator verbs both to see if they were describable through a lens of performance and to ensure that the criterion was the best match for the context and content intent of the draft indicator statement. For example, in our initial draft of the Gateways ECE indicator for Human Growth and Development (HGD1), understands theories of typical and atypical growth in all developmental domains and the interaction between individual and contextual factors on development and learning (Gateways to Opportunity, n.d.), we used the verb "understands." In our analysis for measurability, we asked ourselves how we would describe a practitioner who "understands" human growth and development theory as well as how theory and context interact with individual children and families. Frankly, the obvious sign that we had a measurability issue came from our inability to describe "understanding" in a measurable way that a practitioner could demonstrate. Thus, in our attempts to describe what this competency could look like to a practitioner, we were led to our real intent, that the practitioner could "identify" typical and atypical development regarding physical, social, emotional, and cognitive development and "describe" how individual factors and contextual factors intersect with developmental stages. This verb analysis resulted in rewording the performance indicator HGD1 to, "Identifies and describes (1) theories of typical and atypical growth in all developmental domains and (2) the interaction between individual and contextual factors on development and learning."

Another good example for verb analysis that resulted in performance indicator revision came from the Observation and Assessment competency area. The performance indicator originally stated, "Considers legal and ethical data collection, analysis, and interpretation procedures supportive of child development and learning, program evaluation, and program improvement initiatives" (Gateways to Opportunity, n.d.).

Originally, we drafted the verb "considers," but when trying to describe what a practitioner would demonstrate if they were "considering" legal and ethical procedures, we realized competency was more accurately illustrated by the practitioner's ability to "articulate legal and ethical procedures and 'advocate' for their usage in both program evaluation and improvement contexts."

In these examples, analyzing verbs independently for measurability in and of themselves resulted in verb language changes that better described, observed, defined, or captured performance. Thus, studying indicator verbs for measurability is an essential task in ascertaining the overall measurability of performance indicator statements.

The Illinois ECE competency work accomplished this by targeting one statement that described what indicator performance would actually look like. For the following indicator under the larger competency area of Interactions, Relationships, and Environments (IRE), indicator IRE1 states, "Describes the role of the environment in supporting children's development." This is a simple but vital performance indicator for early childhood practitioners and although the statement is simple, its content is complex. What specific environmental factors can a practitioner actually describe and make a direct connection to supporting children's development? We decided in describing this indicator that "environment" had to be inclusive of both indoor and outdoor learning environments as well as individual developmental and group developmental considerations. We also determined that "supporting" children's development encompassed environmental choices that promoted learning as well as social and emotional development (the classroom community environment). Lastly, we decided on specific environmental elements we should be able to see in a teacher's consideration. These included physical arrangement; materials chosen; organization; accessibility; written and verbal messaging; and images selected. "Describing" this indicator resulted in the authoring of the following performance criteria: "Indoor and outdoor environmental choices support children's learning and create a supportive classroom community by considering individual learner and group needs in regard to:

- physical arrangement
- materials
- organization
- accessibility
- written and verbal messaging
- images

Table 4.1 provides an example of the scoring tool created for the lower level performance indicator IRE1. Using the previous performance criteria—and because the use of "describing" here is more lower level—we decided evaluating this indicator required knowing if they could or could not describe the very specific elements we outlined in the descriptor, as opposed to establishing ranges of description quality like one might see in a leveled scoring tool. We developed a binary scoring tool that can be used to evaluate a teacher's ability to describe environmental choices both indoor and outdoor, across the developmental increments (age 0–3, age 3–5, and kindergarten through third grade), and across the six environmental elements we established in the previous criterion.

In another example, also from the Interactions, Relationships, and Environments competency area, the performance indicator IRE4 states, "Designs learning environments and activities supportive of healthy development and learning." Because this is a higher level verb ("designs"), we felt it was important in this performance criterion to think about what exactly should be included in a competent environmental design for young learners. What does competent environmental design include that supports learning in developmentally appropriate ways for the age of the learners? What types of activities might you see? As you can see in the performance criterion created for this indicator as follows, we established that "designing" should include the ability to incorporate knowledge of development, reflect that knowledge in their environmental design, and show evidence of attention to children's learning and social/emotional needs. This resulted in the following performance criterion for IRE4: "Incorporates knowledge of developmental, individual, and culturally appropriate practice to design environments and activities which are supportive of healthy development and learning, reflective of individual children's needs, and supportive of positive expression of emotions, exploration, and problem-solving."

We determined the performance indicator IRE4 was best measured by using the baseline performance criterion statement as the "meets" level of performance expectation and then describing from there a range of environmental designs from exceptional to unacceptable. Drafting the range of performance language grounded in the performance criteria serves as another filter. If it is difficult to describe the indicator in ranges of performance, revision is needed to truly capture intended performance by strengthening the indicators and criteria. The resulting leveled scoring tool for IRE4 is provided in Table 4.2.

It is obvious with the two indicators exampled here that the lower level indicator (IRE1) is foundational to successful demonstration of the higher level indicator (IRE4). In later steps we will use this leveling of the indicators,

TABLE 4.1
ECE Interactions, Relationships, and Environment (IRE1) Binary Scoring Tool

Indicator	Performance Criteria				Unable to Assess
	O–3	3–5	K–3		
IRE1: Describes the role of the environment in supporting children's development				How indoor environmental choices consider children's development (individual and group)	
				arrangement	
				materials	
				organization and accessibility	
				written and verbal messaging	
				images	
Possible Codes: D = describes, EX = provides example	O–3	3–5	K–3	How indoor environmental choices support children's learning (individual and group)	
				arrangement	
				materials	
				organization and accessibility	
				written and verbal messaging	
				images	
NAEYC: 1d, 4c (1d-LVL1-2, 4c-LVL1-2) IPTS: 4A, 4D InTASC: 3(i), 5(s)	O–3	3–5	K–3	How indoor environmental choices build classroom community	
				arrangement	
				materials	
				organization and accessibility	
				written and verbal messaging	
				images	

(Continues)

Table 4.1 (Continued)

Indicator	Performance Criteria			Unable to Assess
	O–3	3–5	K–3	
			How outdoor environmental choices consider children's development (individual and group)	
			arrangement	
			materials	
			organization and accessibility	
			written and verbal messaging	
			How outdoor environmental choices support children's learning (individual and group)	
			arrangement	
			materials	
			organization and accessibility	
			written and verbal messaging	
			How outdoor environmental choices build classroom community	
			arrangement	
			materials	
			organization and accessibility	
			written and verbal messaging	

From Gateways to Opportunity, *ECE Toolbox*, n.d.

TABLE 4.2
ECE Interactions, Relationships, and Environments Leveled Scoring Tool

Indicator	Distinguished	Competent	Developing	Unacceptable	Unable to Assess
IRE4: Designs learning environments and activities supportive of healthy development and learning NAEYC: 4c (4cLVL1-1) IPTS: 1H, 1K, 1L, 4I, 4J, 4K, 4L InTASC: 1(b), 1(h), 3(f), 3(k)	Incorporates, advocates, and models DAP and input from children to design environments and activities which accommodate individual children's needs and encourage positive expression of emotions, exploration, and problem-solving Environmental design reflects knowledge of legal and ethical principles related to behavior management	Incorporates knowledge of developmental, individual, and culturally appropriate practice to design environments and activities which are supportive of healthy development and learning, reflective of individual children's needs, and supportive of positive expression of emotions, exploration, and problem-solving	Incorporates knowledge of developmental, individual, and culturally appropriate practice to design environments and activities which are supportive of healthy development and learning Explicit attention to individual and group not evident	Learning environments and activities designed are not supportive of healthy development and learning	

From Gateways to Opportunity, *ECE Toolbox*, n.d.

from foundational, within each competency area to advance the operationalizing of competencies into practice. Please note that drafting and articulating performance criteria for indicators provides a critical opportunity to refine and revise the performance indicator statements developed in Step 3. If it is a struggle to actually measure the indicator as written, to come up with a statement that truly captures how you will know it when you see it in practice, it probably means the indicator language needs to be revised.

After performance criteria and subsequent scoring tools were created for each of our draft ECE performance indicators, they were distributed and presented to a wide variety of expert groups, professional organizations, employers, early childhood professional preparation entities, and ECE advocacy and policymaking groups in Illinois. Feedback was collected, analyzed, and presented to the ECE Competency Leadership Team. The leadership team made specific recommendations on how feedback should be incorporated.

Building From a Blueprint: The Tennessee LTSS Story

A key tenet of the Tennessee LTSS example is that training offerings require demonstration of the knowledge, skills, and intellectual behaviors that define each competency area. Completion of the content through participation is not enough—demonstration in a real-to-life context is necessary. This begins with clear and consistent performance expectations with an opportunity for the learner to respond in an authentic workplace situation. To describe what performance looks like and what the learner expectations are for demonstration, levels of mastery across employment roles were created in Step 3 to behaviorally define performance across varying degrees of employment expectations in respective competency areas. The performance indicators described through the levels of mastery are then used to drive the creation of performance criteria.

At this point, clear performance indicators guided the creation of summative level scoring tools with respective criteria. For each competency area, TQI worked with SMEs to create a behavioral data recording tool and corresponding scoring rubric used to evaluate learner performance. In order to create measurement criteria for each competency area, the LTSS process included analyzing the verbs chosen for the performance indicators. Each performance indicator describes expected behavior at the respective level of performance. In turn, the performance indicator must be represented by a verb that accurately aligns to the appropriate level of learning expected and the relative assessment type that will be used to measure it. In other words, does the statement and, more importantly, the verb operationally define

"What does it look like in practice?," "If you saw an effective performer showing the behavior, what are they doing?," and "If you saw a poor performer who needs further development, what are they doing?"

In a framework origin build, the program is built on the foundation of established industry standards. From that point, work to identify an accurate verb happens organically. For LTSS, levels of performance were created and refined through collaboration between a curriculum designer with assessment experience and SMEs. The performance indicators were written through a process in which SMEs answered in descriptive terms, "What does it look like in practice?," and a curriculum designer used the descriptions to create discrete performance criteria. Once created, these performance criteria were workshopped throughout the review and revision process described in Step 3 to ensure alignment to workforce expectations at the corresponding levels.

When building the competency program from established standards, there's a blank canvas for designing intentionally from the start. Evaluating competency for each area allows for the drafting of criteria that describe performance across multiple levels in a way that defines increased sophistication across respective levels. In other words, a higher level of performance is expected at higher levels of competency. For example, in our LTSS work, performance criteria at a lower level of competency, such as "Falls Short," tend to align with the learner's ability to show lower levels of learning, such as "Identifies" or "Recognizes," but the learner is not yet able to show the application or demonstration of those knowledge and skills. Performance criteria at a higher level of competency, such as "Proficient," tend to align with higher levels of learning, such as "Applies" or "Demonstrates." It is important to note that lower levels of competency also describe the presence of undesired behavior. In the LTSS Communication competency, for example, eye-rolling or interrupting is the presence of behavior that indicates the need for development. In the LTSS story, an example of a behavior indicator at the "Falls Short" level includes "Interacts with inappropriate cues, such as eye-rolling or flat affect," while an example of a behavior indicator at the "Proficient" level includes "Communicates in a respectful manner with the person supported, peers, supervisor, etc., such as the use of person-first language and speaking at eye level."

These scoring tools with clear and predetermined criteria are used to evaluate behavior systematically, including the following:

- Certified assessors (trained to record behavioral data in an objective manner) record behavioral data based on objective direct observation of learner behavior. See Figure 4.1 (please note that this example is an excerpt of behavioral data and not the data capture).

Figure 4.1. Excerpt example of assessor notes on behavior.

Assessor Notes on Behavior:

Total Time of Meeting: approx. 13 min 40 s

Nonverbal - eye contact, appears engaged, leaned forward, smiles and recognizes the nonverbal behavior of others (person supported), makes gesture to support explanations (e.g., from the waist up - moves hands from waist up)

Verbal

DSW (D) greets Mr. Bedria (A) and son George (S) - Hello Mr. Bedria and George, It's a pleasure to see you again

D - Want to check in and see how things are going

S interrupts D and speaks for A about stroke

D listens and stops talking to listen when A and S talk

A explains he's embarrassed and doesn't pay own bills

- The behavioral data is sorted along a rating scale according to discrete behaviors that indicate demonstration of the competency area(s). See Figure 4.2 (please note that this example is an excerpt of the rating scale and not the full scoring tool).
- The behavioral data is mapped against predetermined criteria to determine mastery of the competency. See Figure 4.3 (please note that this example is an excerpt of predetermined criteria and not the full rubric tool).

The measurement process outlined previously and the respective tools shown will serve to measure individual or bundles of competencies.

Now that the performance criteria for the indicators have been clearly articulated, you can begin to build a strategy for assessment that will eventually drive content development. With clear criteria written for expected performance, you can begin planning what types of workplace situations are relevant for demonstration of those expected behaviors and what formative experiences are required to build the learner to successful performance in those workplace situations. This is another example of working backward. Backward design of the assessment strategy was captured in an Assessment Outline for each competency area and will be discussed in detail in Step 5. The assessment strategy becomes an important component of both summative assessment used as evaluation *of* learning as well as formative assessment

ESTABLISH COMPETENCY MEASURABILITY   81

Figure 4.2. Excerpt example rating scale across discrete behaviors.

Did the DSW . . .

	Very Little	Somewhat	To a great extent
gather information about ability, needs, wants, and preferences?			X
offer choices based on person's ability, needs, wants, and preferences?			X
encourage independence and voice?			X
advocate for person's voice when needed?		X	
support informed and self-directed decisions?			X
inform of rights and protections?		X	
work with person and family to create suggested goals?		X	

Figure 4.3. Excerpt example of scoring tool with predetermined criteria.

Competency Area: Communication		
Definition: The DSW builds trust and productive relationships with people s/he supports, coworkers and others through respectful and clear verbal and written communication.		
Falls Short	**Proficient**	**Advanced**
• Shows inappropriate cues when interacting with others (e.g., eye-rolling, flat affect) • Rarely demonstrates active listening skills (e.g., clarifying questions, validating comments, leaning forward, head nodding, eye contact)	• Communicates in a respectful manner with the person supported, peers, supervisor, and so on. • Uses person-first language • Keeps personal information confidential when appropriate	• Adapts behavior based on cues • Interacts with positive facial expressions and body language (e.g., eye contact) • Actively encourages and supports the person to take a lead role in her support and/or support team meetings

used as activities *for* learning. Each of these activities, whether formative or summative, require criteria that correspond with the expected level of learning at that point in the development journey.

Points of Intersection: Illinois and Tennessee

The tasks in Step 4 provide an opportunity for individuals and groups creating competencies to refine and revise the draft performance indicators created in Step 3. For example, categorizing indicator verbs by lower and higher level provides a clear lens with which to determine if the verb actually reflects the expectations of the indicator. This perspective allowed us to revise verbs or content language to tighten up or more accurately communicate the intended performance.

In some CBE/CBL efforts it can easily feel like the process is complete with the drafting of the performance indicator statement (Step 3) and in Step 4 you are moving on to "using" or implementing the performance indicators as you examine how the indicator will be measured. However, determining, defining, describing, and analyzing the measurability of each indicator created a solid, measurable foundation for the polishing and honing of our draft indicators. Step 4 also provided the assessment and evaluation foundation for the entire CBE/CBL system. Time invested in the measurability of the indicators allows them to be the underpinning of professional preparation and development, individual performance evaluation, and a larger CBE/CBL program evaluation.

Appendix 4A

 YOUR TURN

Step 1: Analyzing Your Indicator Verbs

Using Table 4.3, list each of your draft performance indicators and code the indicator verb as lower level or higher level. List the verbs (alone) from your performance indicator statements.

Specifically examine the verbs. Are any vague, difficult to picture in action, or complicated to describe? (Avoid vague verbs such as "understands, knows, appreciates, explores," etc.) Revise any vague verbs that do not best support your indicator content. Two examples are provided as follows to get you started. Add rows as needed for your performance indicators.

ESTABLISH COMPETENCY MEASURABILITY 83

TABLE 4.3
Analyze Performance Indicator Verbs

Draft Performance Indicator	Lower Level Verb	Higher Level Verb
IRE1: Describes the role of the environment in supporting children's development	Describes	
IRE4: Designs learning environments and activities supportive of healthy development and learning		Designs

Step 2: Creating Lower Level Performance Criteria

Copy the indicators that you coded as "lower level" into Table 4.4 and list exactly what competent practitioners will name, define, identify, and so forth (depending on your verb). When you look at the object/target of the indicator's verb, how can you break it down into a list of exactly what you will be looking for? Lower level performance indicators should be easily described as knowing/not knowing items listed in the indicator statement or able to achieve/not achieve skills listed in the indicator statement.

TABLE 4.4
Developing Lower Level Verb Performance Criteria

Performance Indicator	Performance Criterion
IRE1: Describes the role of the environment in supporting children's development	Indoor and outdoor environmental choices support children's learning and create a supportive classroom community by considering individual learner and group needs in regard to: • physical arrangement • materials • organization • accessibility • written and verbal messaging • images

Step 3: Create Higher Level Performance Criteria

Copy the indicators that you coded as "higher level" into the Table 4.5 and describe exactly what the object of your indicator verb will look like, contain, or include. When you look at the object/target of the indicator's verb how can you describe exactly what you will be looking for? Can you describe what acceptable performance or demonstration for this indicator in a practicing professional looks like? Can you describe this performance at varying levels?

TABLE 4.5
Developing Higher Level Verb Performance Criterion

Performance Indicator	Performance Criterion
IRE4: Designs learning environments and activities supportive of healthy development and learning	(Design) incorporates knowledge of developmental, individual, and culturally appropriate practice to design environments and activities which are supportive of healthy development and learning, reflective of individual children's needs, and supportive of positive expression of emotions, exploration, and problem-solving

Step 4: Create Binary Scoring Tools

For each lower level indicator, develop a binary scoring tool using the specific elements you identified as essential in the performance description. Table 4.6 provides one template example for a binary scoring tool you could use, reproduce, and modify for each of your lower level indicators. Don't forget to think about ways data could be collected, broken down, and coded in the richest ways.

Step 5: Create Leveled Scoring Tools

For each higher level indicator, develop a leveled scoring tool using the performance description you developed as a plumb line description for average performance and then developing ranges of performance from that baseline description. Table 4.7 provides one template example for a leveled scoring tool you could use, reproduce, and modify for each of your higher level indicators.

ESTABLISH COMPETENCY MEASURABILITY 85

TABLE 4.6
Developing Higher Level Verb Performance Criterion Binary Scoring Tool

Performance Indicator													
Performance Indicator Coding Ideas	Criterion/Element 1			Criterion/Element 2			Criterion/Element 3			Criterion/Element 4			
	Element 1 Subtarget 1	Element 2 Subtarget 2	Element 3 Subtarget 3	Element 1 Subtarget 1	Element 2 Subtarget 2	Element 3 Subtarget 3	Element 1 Subtarget 1	Element 2 Subtarget 2	Element 3 Subtarget 3	Element 1 Subtarget 1	Element 2 Subtarget 2	Element 3 Subtarget 3	

TABLE 4.7
Leveled Scoring Tool Template

Performance Indicator	Distinguished	Competent	Developing	Unacceptable	Unable to Assess
List your performance indicator here (only one indicator per rubric row)		Start by pasting the performance description you developed for this indicator here. Then develop descriptions for "levels" of performance from there			

Step 6: Scoring Tool Reflection and Feedback

Using Table 4.8, assign how and by whom performance descriptions and subsequent evaluation tools will be reviewed by experts and stakeholders. Feedback received should also be tracked as well.

TABLE 4.8
Plan for Scoring Tool Reflection and Feedback

Performance Indicator	Assigned to	Review Requested	Review Completed	Feedback/ Suggestions	Revisions Completed

References

Cooper, J. O., Heron, T. E., & Heward, W. L. (2019). *Applied behavioral analysis* (3rd ed.). Hoboken, NJ: Pearson Education.

Gateways to Opportunity. (n.d.). *ECE toolbox.* https://www.ilgateways.com/professional-development/higher-education-programs/ece-toolbox

Nock, M. K., & Kurtz, S. M. (2005). Direct behavioral observation in school settings: Bringing science to practice. *Cognitive and Behavioral Practice, 12*(3), 359–370. https://doi.org/10.1016/S1077-7229(05)80058-6

Step 5

DEVELOP COMPETENCY ASSESSMENTS

 *Central Question: What is the evidence of competence?*

In Step 4, we described how the draft performance indicators would actually be measured by creating performance criteria that specifically describe how you will know competence when you see it and what a professional will know or be able to do that clearly indicates competence. These provided a base to create assessment experiences for each indicator or group of indicators.

In Step 5, we turn to the actual competency assessment experience. At this point in the CDPM, performance indicators defining competency are becoming finalized, with less substantive revisions occurring. However, subsequent steps in our CDPM may still necessitate some further revision, as every piece in this process can serve to perfect the performance indicators. Step 5, assessing competencies, allows us to examine how performance indicators lend themselves to being assessed. This inspection puts draft performance indicators into a new filter, which again can and should result in some refinement of content and perhaps sequencing. Thus, this next step in the process determines assessment experiences that will produce evidence to measure/assess performance. It is important to note here that assessment experiences are not established *first*. Initially, the measurability is defined in a performance criterion reflecting professional behavior and expectations. This serves to refine and strengthen the performance indicator itself and sets the foundation for substantive indicator assessment.

To help to ensure that assessments are aligned with and truly measure the draft competency areas, as well as designed to meet workforce needs, Step 5 is accomplished by the following:

- determining the assessment experiences needed in each competency area
- creating assessment experiences that generate evidence that can be measured with the scoring tools developed
- matching the scoring tool to assessment experiences
- packaging assessments in ways usable to the field
- reviewing and seeking feedback on assessment experiences

Determine Assessment Experiences Needed for Each Competency Area

For each competency area, it is important to first examine the performance indicators, the sequencing of indicators within the area, and the scoring tools (binary and/or leveled tools) for that competency area. This will help you in determining if assessment experiences for each competency area also need to be leveled or if experiences that are more all-inclusive of the total competency area could be drafted.

As discussed in Step 3, the basic levels of employment in the field were used to level competency. Again, that question, "At what level of employment is this performance indicator necessary?" helps to determine how the indicators would be sequenced. This understanding has been important throughout this process and is also relevant here as we develop assessment experiences. Assessment experiences can be developed to produce evidence as to competency for individual indicators or multiple indicators in a competency area. Competency can be captured together via one assessment experience based on performance indicators that are interrelated or based on a targeted employment level.

Creating Assessment Experiences That Produce Measurable Evidence

At this point, it is necessary to build assessment experiences with specific instructions. These assessment experiences should be able to produce evidence of measurable knowledge, skills, and intellectual behaviors. The exercise of constructing these assessment experiences serves as a final refining point for draft performance indicators. With the completion of Step 4, you should have determined that each indicator is indeed assessable. Measurability is operationalized through the creation of the scoring tool (binary or leveled). As you create the assessment experiences, you are provided an opportunity to revise or clarify the draft performance indicators. It is possible that some indicators may prove difficult to "capture" in evidentiary ways. This does not make them unimportant; however, they may need to be revised, be rethought, or display evidence in a unique way. For example, many professional dispositions (e.g., integrity, ethics, etc.) are examples of competency areas that, while very important, are difficult to capture in evidentiary ways through a prescribed assessment experience.

Matching Scoring Tools to Assessment Experiences

The indicators and development of the scoring tools (binary or leveled) for the competencies guide the creation of the assessment experiences. Now each experience must be looped back and matched with the appropriate scoring tools. This link should be logical, meaning that assessment experiences created in the name of specific indicators should easily match to the scoring tools for those indicators. If the evidence envisioned by the completion of the assessment experience cannot be evaluated using the corresponding scoring tool, this is a final opportunity to revise/refine the experience or scoring tool or perhaps the indicator itself.

Structuring or Packaging Assessment Experiences Based on Field Expectations

Once assessment experiences have been drafted and matched with the corresponding scoring tools, they should be packaged for use in both professional preparation and professional development. Will each performance indicator be assessed individually? Will experiences, and subsequently indicators, be bundled by mastery or employment level? This "packaging" is one of the final tests for the draft performance indicators. In beginning to operationalize them, some final revisions may need to be made.

Assessment Experience Review

Using stakeholder groups established in Step 3, assessment experiences and aligned scoring tools should be vetted through expert groups that represent all stakeholders (e.g., employers, professional organizations, oversight agencies, etc.) as well as both field preparation and professional development providers.

Remodeling the House: The Illinois ECE Story

In our Illinois story, constructing assessment experiences needed to provide rigorous evidence of the indicator while allowing statewide program autonomy in their construction and "bundling." For example, the performance indicators related to working with family and community relationships (FCR) were sequenced beginning with FCR1, "Outlines the role and influence of families and communities on children's development, learning, and the early childhood setting," which is essential for the teacher assistant level and anyone working with young children. At the other end of this professional theme, FCR7, "Designs and advocates for procedures, plans, and policies that inform child and program goals, in collaboration with families and other team members," obviously articulates an expectation of competence at a much higher teacher leader level as the professional is *creating* policy and systems. In developing and "packaging" assessment experiences, it was essential in each competency area to understand mastery levels within the profession (see Table 5.1).

TABLE 5.1
Gateways Competencies Assessed

Teacher Assistant	**ECE FCR1**: Outlines the role and influence of families and communities on children's development, learning, and the early childhood setting
Teacher	**ECE FCR4**: Identifies, selects, and promotes meaningful connections to community resources that are responsive to the unique strengths, priorities, concerns, and needs of young children and their families
	ECE FCR5: Describes culturally and linguistically responsive communication and collaboration strategies, which facilitate culturally sensitive expectations for children's development and learning and family engagement in assessment and goal setting
	ECE FCR6: Selects and implements culturally and linguistically appropriate procedures designed to gather information about children and families, including child and family strengths, priorities, concerns, and needs, and collaboratively integrates this information into child and family goals
Teacher Leader	**ECE FCR7**: Designs and advocates for procedures, plans, and policies, informing child and program goals, in collaboration with families and other team members

Understanding and visualizing leveling through a lens of professional practice is essential to designing assessments that measure a professional's competence. It is obvious, in this example, that one assessment experience targeting all seven of these FCR competencies would not be useful, fair, or needed for the teacher assistant level. It is, however, essential that the teacher leader demonstrate, via an assessment experience, their competence not just in regard to FCR7, but in all seven of the FCR competencies as they all build upon and undergird one another at the teacher leader level.

The assessment experience provided as follows is an Illinois example of a specific experience that we designed to align to applicable performance indicators for Heath, Safety, and Wellness. This first experience is prescriptive and guides the practitioner, at the assistant teacher level (Level 2), in an exercise to produce evidence of his or her competency.

As described in the following experience (Table 5.2), the professional is asked to do an environmental scan of specific, environmentally safe and unsafe practices, procedures, and elements and then to describe and identify policies, procedures, and resources related to best practice in regard to health and safety.

Our leveling of assessment experiences is demonstrated in the continuing example as follows by including all competency expectations up to the level being assessed. Higher level experiences asked the novice teacher (Level 3) not only to provide a safe environment, but also to analyze the environment and make recommendations for safe and healthy procedures (see Table 5.3).

The assessment experience for the Level 4 professional, the classroom teacher, asks the practitioner to take the identified knowledge demonstrated in Level 2 and analyzed in Level 3 and apply that knowledge and analysis through artifact resource collection evidence (see Table 5.4).

Lastly, in the highest level assessment experience for Health, Safety, and Wellness (see Table 5.5), the lead teacher is asked to demonstrate his or her ability to influence and mentor others in healthy and safe environments by developing procedures for classroom/school/center staff to ensure safe practices, as well as to systematically evaluate and support these practices.

These assessment experiences allow us to consistently measure practitioner performance using identified indicators, and the compiled data can also provide, over time, relevant formative and summative preparation program or practitioner evaluation information.

After we drafted assessment experiences that could generate evidence of competency at each level, we matched the tasks with the relative scoring tools we had developed for the HSW performance indicators in Step 4.

TABLE 5.2
HSW Level I Assessment Experience

Part 1: Environmental "Scavenger" Hunt Through your clinical site or other licensed child-care facility, arrange a date and time to visit to complete your environmental Health and Safety Checklist.	**Before your observation:**<ul><li>Locate and study the licensing standards for day-care centers (e.g., in 2019, and in Illinois, this would be Subpart G: Health and Hygiene from the Illinois Department of Children and Family Services [2010, December 15], Licensing standards for day-care centers. (http://www.state.il.us/dcfs/docs/407.pdf). If not there, please search for the most recent version.</li></ul>**During your observation:**<ul><li>Complete the Health and Safety Checklist and the Menu Review Checklist, collecting evidence as available (pictures, if allowed, sketches, examples, menus, documents, etc.)</li></ul>**Postenvironmental Assessment Reflection:**<ul><li>Summarize the results of your completed Health and Safety Checklist. This summary should include the following:<ul><li>An overview of program practices related to:<ul><li>Maintaining regulations, standards, and guidelines for indoor and outdoor environments, food preparation, and handling</li><li>Emergency medical and first aid procedures</li><li>Instructions and required documentation for administration of different medicines and approved medical treatments</li><li>State and local regulations for meal preparation</li><li>Maintaining a healthy, safe, and risk-free environment</li><li>Record keeping</li><li>Reporting child abuse and neglect</li></ul></li><li>A description of how the environment you observed compares to licensing standards provided through the Department</li></ul></li></ul>

Part 2: **Recommendations** Based on data collected, make specific recommendations for each of the following, highlighting key areas of supporting health, nutrition, and safety for young children:	Children • Sample statement that outlines how you would help children understand healthy habits • Sample statement that outlines how you would help children understand personal safety Families • Sample statement for new parents or parents considering this center that outlines your vision and commitment to keeping children healthy and safe Classroom Staff • Three daily procedures in the classroom that promote or strengthen health, safety, and nutrition
Part 3: **Community/Professional Resources** Develop a physical portfolio (this can be a file, notebook, or electronic tool such as a wiki, original website, or live binder) to collect and organize community and professional resource information you could reference and continue to grow with regarding health, safety, and nutrition resources. The binder should have a minimum of six resources and be organized in an easily searchable, useable, editable way, such as:	Health Information Safety Information Nutrition Information

From Gateways to Opportunity, *ECE Toolbox*, n.d.

Note: This assessment will evaluate your ability to assess and analyze specific child/family health and nutrition information with the health, safety, and nutrition policies and procedures of a classroom or program/school/center. You will use this information and your analysis to inform the design and implementation of recommendations you will make.

TABLE 5.3
HSW Level 3 Assessment Task

Part 1: Environmental "Scavenger" Hunt	**Level 2 PLUS:** In your postreflection address: • How children and staff are supported in practicing safe and healthy behaviors through daily routines and activities
Part 2: Recommendations	**Level 2 PLUS:** Recommendations, also include: • One weekly procedure in the classroom that promotes or strengthens health, safety, and nutrition
Part 3: Community/Professional Resources	**Level 3 PLUS:** Community/Professional Resources, should include: • At least 10 total resources

From Gateways to Opportunity, *ECE Toolbox*, n.d.

Note: This assessment will evaluate your ability to assess and analyze specific child/family health and nutrition information with the health, safety and nutrition policies and procedures of a classroom or program/school/center. You will use this information and your analysis to inform the design and implementation of recommendations you will make.

We aligned the following binary scoring tool (see Table 5.6) to assess the competence demonstrated in the evidence produced from the Level 2 HSW task described previously.

Table 5.7 provides an excerpt of the scoring tool developed in Step 4 for the HSW area. The tool is color coded by the levels discussed in the previous assessment experiences. Table 5.7 provides an example of Level 2.

It is important to again emphasize that all evidence produced from the designed experience is measured against the performance indicators using our previously developed scoring tools. The creation of assessment experiences allows practitioners, preparation programs, and evaluators to establish options for providing evidence; what is consistent is the scoring tool. Using scoring tools that center completely on describing performance of the indicator forces assessment of the competency as opposed to "grading" of the experience or other peripheral behaviors, such as grammar, spelling, timely submission, and so on.

In our Illinois example we also developed data analysis tables based on the scoring tool for collection, tracking, and analysis of evaluation data both at larger program levels and over time. This is discussed in detail in Step 7.

TABLE 5.4
HSW Level 4 Assessment Task

Part 1: Environmental "Scavenger" Hunt	**Level 3 PLUS:** In your postreflection address: • What additional information would have been beneficial for you to make a full assessment of health and safety factors within the program you observed?
Part 2: Recommendations	**Level 3 PLUS:** Recommendations, also include: • One monthly procedure in the classroom that promotes or strengthens health, safety, and nutrition
Part 3: Community/ Professional Resources	**Level 3 PLUS:** Community/Professional Resources, should include: • At least 20 total resources

From Gateways to Opportunity, *ECE Toolbox*, n.d.
Note: This assessment will evaluate your ability to assess and analyze specific child/family health and nutrition information with the health, safety, and nutrition policies and procedures of a classroom or program/school/center. You will use this information and your analysis to inform the design and implementation of recommendations you will make.

TABLE 5.5
HSW Level 5 Assessment Task

Part 2: Recommendations	**Level 4 PLUS:** Recommendations, also include: • One annual procedure In the classroom that promotes or strengthens health, safety, and nutrition
Part 3: Community/ Professional Resources	**Level 4 PLUS:** • Community/Professional Resources, should include: • At least 25 total resources

From Gateways to Opportunity, *ECE Toolbox*, n.d.
Note: This assessment will evaluate your ability to assess and analyze specific child/family health and nutrition information with the health, safety, and nutrition policies and procedures of a classroom or program/school/center. You will use this information and your analysis to inform the design and implementation of recommendations you will make.

TABLE 5.6
ECE Health, Safety, and Wellness Level 2 Assessment Checklist

Competency	Checklist Criteria		Unable to Assess
HSW1: Articulates components of a safe and healthy environment NAEYC: 6b (6b-LVL1-3-4) IPTS:4G InTASC: 3(k)	At the classroom level . . .		
		signs of abuse and neglect	
		ways of documenting abuse and neglect	
		steps in reporting abuse and neglect	
		maintenance of a safe and risk-free indoor environment for children in which hazards are identified, risks assessed, and threats responded to with appropriate corrective action	
		food preparation and handling procedures	
		emergency medical and first aid procedures	
		ongoing wellness (providing instructions and required documentation for administration of different medicines and approved medical treatments and heath appraisals)	
		contagious disease prevention	
		contagious disease procedures	
		nutritional practices	
		record-keeping related to health and safety (risk analysis documentation, accident reports, etc.)	
		standards and regulations related to health and safety	

W2: Maintains a safe and healthy environment	At the classroom level . . .								
	documents abuse and neglect								
	follows steps in reporting abuse and neglect								
NAEYC: 1d, 6b (1d-LVL1-2, 6b-LVL1-3) IPTS:4I InTASC: 3(k)	maintains a safe and risk-free indoor environment for children in which hazards are identified, risks assessed, and threats responded to with appropriate corrective action								
	follows food preparation and handling procedures								
	follows emergency medical and first aid procedures								
	follows ongoing wellness procedures (providing instructions and required documentation for administration of different medicines and approved medical treatments and heath appraisals)								
	follows contagious disease prevention procedures								
	follows contagious disease procedures								
	maintains healthy nutritional practices								
	follows record-keeping expectations related to health and safety (risk analysis documentation, accident reports, etc.)								
	follows standards and regulations related to health and safety								

From Gateways to Opportunity, *ECE Toolbox*, n.d.

TABLE 5.7
ECE Health, Safety, and Wellness Level 2 Scoring Tool

Competency	Competent	Unable to Assess
ECE Health, Safety, and Wellness Master Rubric		
Competency	**Competent** / **Checklist Criteria**	**Unable to Assess**
HSW1: Articulates components of a safe and healthy environment **NAEYC:** 6b (6b-LVL1-3-4) **IPTS:** 4G **InTASC:** 3(k)	At the classroom level . . .	
	signs of abuse and neglect	
	ways of documenting abuse and neglect	
	steps in reporting abuse and neglect	
	maintenance of a safe and risk-free indoor environment for children in which hazards are identified, risks assessed, and threats responded to with appropriate corrective action	
	food preparation and handling procedures	
	emergency medical and first aid procedures	
	ongoing wellness (providing instructions and required documentation for administration of different medicines and approved medical treatments and health appraisals)	
	contagious disease prevention	
	contagious disease procedures	
	nutritional practices	
	record-keeping related to health and safety (risk analysis documentation, accident reports, etc.)	
	standards and regulations related to health and safety	
Competency	**Competent** / **Checklist Criteria**	**Unable to Assess**
HSW2: Maintains a safe and healthy environment **NAEYC:** Id, 6b (Id-LVL1-2.6b-LVL1-3) **IPTS:** 4I **InTASC:** 3(k)	At the classroom level . . .	
	documents abuse and neglect	
	follows steps in reporting abuse and neglect	
	maintains a safe and risk-free indoor environment for children in which hazards are identified, risks assessed, and threats responded to with appropriate corrective action	
	follows food preparation and handling procedures	
	follows emergency medical and first aid procedures	
	follows ongoing wellness procedures (providing instructions and required documentation for administration of different medicines and approved medical treatments and health appraisals)	
	follows contagious disease prevention procedures	
	follows contagious disease procedures	

Competency	Competent		Unable to Assess
	Checklist Criteria		
	maintains healthy nutritional practices		
	follows record-keeping expectations related to health and safety (risk analysis documentation, accident reports, etc.)		
	follows standards and regulations related to health and safety		

From Gateways to Opportunity, *ECE Toolbox*, n.d.

Building From a Blueprint: The Tennessee LTSS Story

After competency definitions have been developed, including performance at respective levels of mastery and corresponding criteria, you now have measurable action statements that appropriately reflect sophistication across levels of performance. This allows for assessment techniques to be identified for expected levels of competency performance. For each of the 12 competency areas, Level 2 – Frontline DSW (direct service worker) was identified as the target level of development and expected performance for the initial QuILTSS WFD learner population. As such, assessments were built to evaluate expected performance at Level 2, although expected performance at Levels 1, 3, and 4 were defined as well. Formative assessment experiences should also be recognized here. Assessment activities that build the learner to performance on summative assessment should be planned for in Stage 2 of the backward design process. The key formative activities that will serve as benchmarks, safe practice opportunities, and stepping stones that scaffold the learner to successful performance should be created in order to design a comprehensive assessment strategy. TQI created an assessment strategy for each competency area. See Figure 5.1 (please note that this example is an excerpt of the assessment outline scale and not the full assessment strategy).

It is important to remember that competencies are defined by what a learner knows and "can do." For the TQI program, performance was defined in the Levels of Mastery through behavior demonstrated in the workplace. Even at Level 1—Not Yet Proficient, both the absence of behavior and, more importantly, the presence of behavior was described. For example, while active listening behavior may be absent at Level 1, there is in turn the presence of distracting behavior, such as interrupting or phone use, that can be measured and demonstrates "lacking" proficient behavior. The intent of evidence in QuILTSS WFD is to predict the likelihood of successful Level 2 performance in the workplace. It is important then that the assessment experiences mirror the workplace as closely as possible. In other words, the learner

Figure 5.1. Excerpt example of assessment outline for cultural competency.

Badge Assessments

1. The learner will self-check for potential barriers such as biases, prejudices, etc.
2. The learner will recognize a culturally sensitive support plan
3. The learner will implement a culturally sensitive support plan across settings, cultural situations (e.g., gender, disability, ethnicity, etc.)

Module Assessments

  Module 1 Assessments: Diversity and Cultural Awareness

    Summative Assessments

- Recognize characteristics, interactions, role of the family, preferences, communication styles, etc. across a variety of cultures
- Assessment Techniques: Interactive videos

    Formative Assessments

- Identify characteristics, interactions, role of the family, preferences, communication styles, etc. across a variety of cultures
  - What are these cultures?
  - What are the characteristics, interactions, role of the family, preferences, communication styles, etc. of these cultures?
  - Why is it important?
- Recognize characteristics, interactions, role of the family, preferences, communication styles, etc. across a variety of cultures
  - What does it look like in practice?
  - How should it be considered in practice?
  - What is the DSW's role?

From The QuiLTSS Institute, n.d.

is dropped into an authentic workplace experience, and the learner's response is then directly observed by a certified assessor and evaluated accordingly using workplace-relevant and predetermined criteria as described in Step 4. The behaviorally based assessment experiences are developed to validate performance at Level 2 and are created through the following steps:

- *Gather field-recruited scenarios.* TQI recruited authentic workplace situations from the field of LTSS.
- *Extract workplace situations that align with opportunities to showcase behaviors expected for required competencies.* TQI used assessment experts to analyze the field-recruited workplace situations against the competency definitions, specifically the Levels of Mastery, to identify situations that provide opportunities for learners to demonstrate predefined behaviors expected at Level 2.
- *Write the simulation scenarios.* TQI used assessment experts to create standardized assessment scenarios for delivery to learners through virtual

simulation software built from the recruited workplace situations. See Figure 5.2 (please note that this example is an excerpt of the standardized delivery template and not the full scenario design tool). Standardization of the simulation scenario is essential to create a fair experience across learners. Part of the standardization process includes explicitly creating guaranteed challenges and opportunities for learners to demonstrate expected behaviors.

Figure 5.2. Excerpt example of standardized delivery template.

Planned Challenges

Challenge 1:
George dominates the conversation.

Performance Objective 1:
Gain understanding of Mr. Sera's goals, needs, and preferences and redirect the conversation.

When learner . . .	Avatars will . . .
HIT	HIT
Speaks articulately Asks open-ended questions Directs questions at Mr. Sera Shows active listening skills Shows support Uses first-person language	(Donald) Talk about how much he loved his work Talk about enjoying coworkers and having friends Mention becoming lonely since stroke and retirement
MISS	MISS
Does not articulate ideas clearly Does not ask open-ended questions Does not ask about goals or preferences Does not appear supportive Directs questions at George	(Donald) Be hesitant to share details Shut down (George) Speak for Donald

---

From The QuiLTSS Institute, n.d.

- *Write role and supporting information for each simulation participant.* TQI required trained simulation specialists (professional actors trained to power avatars in the simulation software) to be certified on each simulation scenario to ensure consistent scenario delivery to learners. As part of the standardized delivery process, explicit instructions are written for each role in the assessment process. A template is used to identify what information the learner, the simulation specialist, and the assessor will receive.
- *Design realistic and consistent experience parameters.* Continuing with the theme of a standardized, consistent, and fair experience for learners,

behavioral hits and misses are created with SMEs. Behavioral hits are defined as desired responses from the learner that result in predetermined responses from the avatar. For example, if the learner demonstrates person-centered, active listening behaviors, such as asking open-ended questions, then the avatar talks about how much he loved his work and that he has become lonely since he had a stroke. Behavioral misses are defined as undesired responses from the learner that result in predetermined responses from the avatar. For example, if the learners demonstrate task-oriented, distracted behaviors, such as asking closed-ended questions, then the avatar is hesitant to share information and the second avatar speaks out of turn.

Assessment experiences are designed to measure multiple competencies at once as needed. For example, one assessment experience allows for evaluation of four competency areas such as Communication, Person-Centered Practices, Evaluation and Observation, and Professionalism and Ethics. In this way, a learner can work through the content and demonstrate competence in four competency areas through one assessment experience. The technology used to power TQI's simulation exercises can be further explored at https://www.mursion.com/.

In the Tennessee LTSS story, the scoring tools, including behavioral data recording tools and rubrics, were custom created for Level 2 evaluation of each competency area. While the assessment experience is designed to measure multiple competency areas simultaneously, each competency area is evaluated at the individual level, meaning each competency area has its own scoring rubric. This means it is possible to evaluate one competency area in isolation as well as multiple competencies simultaneously.

In the LTSS story, the 12 competencies are packaged into three bundles of four competency areas. The bundles were created as a suggested sequence of courses, each bundle intended to be a 6-credit hour semester when taken through a partner postsecondary institution. Field experts suggested this bundling, which begins with foundational concepts, such as Communication, and progresses through seemingly more advanced competency areas, such as Cultural Competency, that build off of those that come before it. As described in Step 2, the DSW works through the career pathway with the four-course bundles and receives a pay increase as they successfully complete the required demonstration of those competency areas.

In the TQI story, key stakeholders should be involved in the process of vetting the assessment experiences and respective measurement tools. To accomplish this, the following steps were taken:

- *Workshopping the assessment experience:* TQI used a certified simulation specialist to deliver the standardized simulation scenario(s) to SMEs. The SMEs acted as the learner in the scenario, providing a good performance and a poor performance within the workplace situation based on common behaviors in the field. The SMEs verified authenticity of the assessment experience by providing feedback on the simulation scenarios and scoring tools, and revisions were made as necessary.
- *Piloting the assessment experience:* TQI beta-tested the assessment experience with learners recruited from the field of LTSS. Based on learner performance and feedback, revisions were made accordingly.
- *Launching simulation with learners:* TQI was ready to launch the Level 2 assessment experiences with learners in the WFD program.

The assessment experiences and corresponding scoring tools are significant to the continuous improvement process as feedback should continuously be sought, considered, and applied as necessary.

Points of Intersection: Illinois and Tennessee

Draft performance indicators are reaching a point now in the CDPM where revisions should be minor and limited to sharpening their wording or usability. After examining stakeholder feedback received on assessment drafts, evidence produced, and linked measurement tools, you should conclude any revisions as needed. Remember the domino effect of revision at this point. Most revision needed on assessment tasks could and very probably will lead to revision of the corresponding measurement tool and aligned performance indicator.

In the development of your performance indicators, it feels more natural to jump from an indicator statement straight to what a practitioner should do to prove they know or can do what the statement is describing. In that sequence, assessment of the performance indicator is considered through the lens of the task and becomes an assessment of ability to perform that specific task (or grading) as opposed to clear assessment of level or degree of competency. In contrast to this typical approach, the CDPM emphasizes the importance of designing performance indicator measurement tools first (Step 4) and then considering the many possible ways that competency could be shown, all using the same measurement tool. This allows for deeper assessment of actual competency and provides clear direction for specific next steps in professional practice or program improvement.

Appendix 5A

 **YOUR TURN**

Given the previous directives, answer the following questions:
What specific tasks will you design that produce outputs or evidence that can be measured using the scoring tools created in Step 5?

TABLE 5.8
Overview of Assessment Tasks Reflective of Performance Indicators

Assessment Task Summary	Performance Indicator(s) Assessed

Guiding Questions:
- How will these tasks be organized to represent competency expectations regarding scope, sequencing, and leveling?
- How can assessment tasks be potentially "stacked," assessing lower level or more general competency and stacking to higher level more complex competency?
- How can assessments be used or organized for a variety of preparation or professional development contexts?
- In what ways has the creation of the assessment tasks revealed a need to revise any performance indicators, scope or sequence, framework elements, or organization?

Reference

Gateways to Opportunity. (n.d.). *ECE toolbox.* https://www.ilgateways.com/professional-development/higher-education-programs/ece-toolbox

Step 6

ADOPT AND IMPLEMENT COMPETENCIES IN THE LEARNING JOURNEY AND CREDENTIALING SYSTEMS

Central Question: What processes will be needed to anchor competencies in education and workforce contexts?

During Stage 3 of backward design, a learning journey is constructed that explicitly builds the learner to successful demonstration of each competency. During this phase of our CDPM, all the hard work that has gone into establishing your competency framework, competency areas, and performance indicators comes to life through the construction of a learning journey. The learning journey clearly builds the learner to the predetermined end or expected outcomes. Well-developed competency-based models can be meaningful within education and workforce contexts. The process of developing a competency-based model requires partnership with key stakeholders, including employers, practitioners, students, and academic institution personnel such as faculty, course designers, and program designers (Sanden et al., 2016). Step 6 of the CDPM emphasizes the process of ensuring the meaningful integration of competencies within education and workforce contexts. As with the other chapters, applied examples from the states of Illinois and Tennessee are used to illustrate key points.

The holistic impact of competency-based performance indicators on education and workforce contexts is informed by stakeholder input. This input serves to map the impact of competencies on preservice and in-service professionals, employment requirements, performance evaluation, program evaluation, and policies and procedures, and is critical to ensuring that the competency performance indicators developed are meaningful, relevant, and used in professional practice. The impact of attaining this input from three different types of relevant stakeholders is detailed as follows.

Employers

When competency-based models are designed well, employers are provided with assurances that higher education program graduates have the knowledge, skills, and intellectual behaviors needed for their positions. Such assertions result from rich partnerships with employers that inform both competency content and systemic competency integration throughout educational institutions, career pathways, and the workplace (Klein-Collins, 2013).

The goal of systemic competency integration is the creation of a seamless, continuous system, where competency performance indicators first embedded within educational institutions are then reflected in the broader field or vice versa. Within this system, the learning journey is based on student/practitioner skill development that promotes successful performance of their targeted workforce role(s). The application of competencies within the workforce context ensures these same skills are embedded within workplace evaluation, mentorship, and continuous professional development. Furthermore, a well-developed competency-based system based on a career pathway approach is overt and easy to understand: Those *entering* the field clearly comprehend the knowledge, skills, and intellectual behaviors needed, those *already in* the field know how to progress to new roles, and workforce and educational contexts have a shared understanding of how to support individuals in developing and refining essential proficiencies (Smither et al., 2016).

As noted in the introduction to this volume, the benefits of competency-based models include transparency, accountability, portability, and comparability of student knowledge, skills, and intellectual behaviors (Book, 2014). Factors such as transparency and accountability may be particularly advantageous to employers, as there can be assurances that prerequisite knowledge, skills, and intellectual behaviors are embedded within an easy-to-understand model that includes robust assessment strategies. Accountability can also be fostered through clarity in role expectations, reflecting a clear understanding of competencies for employees, based on credential or degree attainment. Each of these factors may be advantageous for pre- and in-service professionals as well.

Pre- and In-Service Professionals

Well-developed competency-based models are transparent and easy to understand (Phillips & Schneider, 2016). This is particularly true when competencies are arranged in a career pathway model that clearly communicates targeted knowledge, skills, intellectual behaviors, and workforce outcomes. Clarity in communication can also support articulation as institutions have the capacity to understand targeted knowledge, skills, and intellectual behaviors and how these were measured. In addition, competency-based models may support portability as competencies can be clearly defined and agreed upon. For example, when competencies are utilized, students who swirl between institutions or exit and restart studies are not as vulnerable to factors such as credit loss and additional time to degree. Additionally, completed workforce training follows participants to subsequent or concurrent employers. Transparency, the logical sequencing of coursework, free of hidden prerequisites and requirements, and portability, the ability to transfer credits, complete degrees, and continue degrees at other institutions, can also support student progress within his or her chosen field, as the career pathway model identifies specific competencies needed to further develop within the profession.

Educational Institutions

Clear expectations, as well as guidelines on how to assess program and course requirements, support institution flexibility. The established competency foundation can provide educational institutions with a means of ensuring parity in both content and measurement across unique delivery systems. For example, coursework at the community college and 4-year institution that cover and measure the same competency areas can allow for course credit and assessment data to be portable between institutions. With that in mind, an aligned competency system can allow institutions to have assessment data (based on competency) at all levels on all students.

The competency mapping process outlined provides a holistic overview of opportunities for systemic integration of competencies. At this point, it is important to explore the implications for professional preparation requirements, the learning journey defined by those requirements, and workforce performance expectations. The entirety of preparation pathways and related learning journeys leading to the workforce context, and professional development opportunities within the workplace, need to be considered. A key question to consider is how the integration of competencies will influence existing systems and requirements for practitioners currently working in the field as well as those preparing for employment.

Ideally, performance indicators required for occupational entry and ongoing development represent the professional development system supporting the field. In many cases, requirements for job roles are overt, but specific pathways for ongoing development within one's chosen role are often vague. For example, a field might clearly communicate that a bachelor's degree in a related field is required for employment. However, workforce professional development opportunities often do not reflect individual preferences, goals, or performance needs. The competency-based system needs to encompass the whole of professional development, from selecting a profession, to acquiring competencies, to entering the profession, to developing within that profession.

 Remodeling the House: The Illinois ECE Story

As noted, use of the CDPM within Illinois is based on a career pathway approach. In the Illinois early childhood field, in accordance with recommendations from the Alliance for Quality Career Pathways (2014), a clear sequence of coursework and credentials was constructed from embedded, employer-validated performance indicators. This career pathway model was then linked to industry-recognized credentials and arranged within a career lattice describing core performance indicators that outline the knowledge, skills, and intellectual dispositions needed to enter and progress in the field. Please see the following for an infographic of the model: https://www.siue.edu/ierc/pdf/2017-3_EPPI_Workforce_Infographic.pdf

This remodeling, reflective of the deconstruction-reconstruction approach, presented several advantages, including the potential for parity across the two existing pathways in the field that lead to credentials. One of these pathways was referred to as an entitled pathway, where individuals could attain credentials based on their successful completion of coursework at Gateways-approved higher education institutions. The other pathway, referred to as a direct pathway, was designed for individuals who swirled and accumulated credit from institutions of higher education and had a combination of training and college credit that could apply directly to earn their Gateways credential. In the newly developed competency-based system, opportunities for clarity in pathway requirements and progression were created for those who were already working in the field and those who were preparing to enter the field. This was deemed extremely advantageous by faculty, student, and workforce stakeholders because a clear delineation of competency needed to earn a credential at the state level would promote clarity among all training entities. This clarity also solidified expectations of early childhood professionals at a variety of employment levels, from the paraprofessional (teacher assistant) in the classroom to the program director/leader.

Stakeholder feedback also influenced competency scope and impact as information gathered from these individuals led to a clear understanding of the myriad of opportunities for competency integration within the system. Individuals are trained using a competency-based system that clearly identifies needed knowledge, skills, and intellectual behaviors. Opportunities exist within early childhood programs to create program evaluation tied to professional development. When ongoing professional development reflects competencies, there is ease in identifying related supports that directly reflect employees' strengths and opportunities for growth. Integrating competencies into program evaluation extends this relationship in a similar way, but as opposed to reflecting individual competencies, it reflects targets at the classroom/organizational level. When fully integrated, competencies reflected should be evidenced in handbooks, evaluation tools used, and ongoing professional development supports provided.

As noted, robust competency development processes can be responsive to the professional development needs of practitioners seeking to enter and those who are employed within a targeted field. With that in mind, existing challenges in the Illinois early childhood field, as noted in Step 1 of this volume, are the number of early childhood practitioners who have completed some college education but lack completion of a degree or Gateways Credential and those who have completed a degree or credential but lack specific content knowledge (Illinois Network of Child Care Resource and Referral Agencies, 2014).

Before the development of learning journeys could begin, field-based knowledge of the CDPM was critical. This included developing a toolbox that consisted of a variety of resources supporting assessment within a competency-based system. The toolbox is housed on the Gateways to Opportunity (n.d.) website, and resources include a Webcast Series, Competency Assessment Guide, Overview of Faculty Assessment Project, Example Assessments, and Master Rubrics. The Gateways to Opportunity toolbox webpage provides a variety of helpful resources, each of which are described in the following sections.

Gateways Toolbox Overview

One of the first resources found on the toolbox is a series of webcasts. These "webbies," as they came to be known, were designed for faculty and trainers with an overview of the origins of competencies, their stackability and how they were arranged by credential level, and how competency performance indicators related to curriculum and assessment. A companion to the video information was the Competency Assessment Guide, which was a written compilation of all foundational information included in the webcast series as well as information on how each of the credentials within the Gateways system intersect.

The Gateways toolbox also includes sample assessments by level for each of the competency areas as well as Master Rubrics aligned to competency area and level.

Initial Learning Journey Development

From its inception, the Gateways to Opportunity system included recognition of knowledge, skills, and intellectual behaviors developed in on-the-job training as well as those attained within institutions of higher education. Competencies have the potential to serve as an equalizer or shared currency between credential pathways as a common requirement in demonstrated knowledge, skills, and intellectual behavior. A pilot that demonstrated the range of opportunities competencies provided was implemented at an Illinois community college in the spring of 2017. The pilot included assessment based on prior learning, opportunities to earn credit from field-based training coupled with assessment, and traditional online course materials. Participants were placed in the program based on credentials and college coursework already attained. The individualized nature of content delivery as well as the learning-agnostic components of the model significantly reduced participant cost and time to credential attainment. This learning journey leveraged the existing framework, utilizing backward design to ensure learners were engaged in a clear and relevant pathway supporting successful performance.

Further exploration of a competency-based learning journey based on an adaptation of our CDPM is presently occurring in Illinois with a statewide modularization pilot. The Illinois Governor's Office of Early Childhood Development received federal funds through the Preschool Development Birth to Five (PDG B–5) Renewal Grant and partnered with INCCRRA to offer grant opportunities via RFP to five Illinois higher education institutions to participate in the Gateways to Opportunity ECE Credential competency-based modularization project. The selected 2- and 4-year institutions were provided with an opportunity to innovate and increase accessibility of their early childhood teacher preparation programs through exploration of performance indicators within modularized, competency-based, online accessible minicourse sequences tied to professional development, opportunities for college credit, and the potential to earn credit for prior learning.

 Building From a Blueprint: The Tennessee LTSS Story

To date, the QuILTSS Institute has developed 22 different competency-based courses, which can be taken individually, in predetermined blocks, or through a more comprehensive program. All of the courses have been modularized, so smaller "chunks" of content can be regrouped into new courses. This modularization will allow the institute to quickly modify its proposed course based on the needs of the learner population.

The 12 courses in the WFD program have all been created to allow individuals to earn college credits as courses are successfully completed. Through a master service agreement in place between TQI, the TBR, and participating Tennessee community colleges and colleges of applied technology, individuals could earn up to 18 college credits in less than 1 year. Participating Tennessee institutions will enroll and award college credit for TQI badges for out-of-state students too. Therefore, it was necessary that the learning journey was built with both workforce needs as well as educational requirements in mind. For example, ensuring substantive interaction initiated by faculty is necessary in order to award college-level credit.

When a learner demonstrates competence in all 12 workforce development areas and earns the respective badges, these weave together into the full QuILTSS credential. (See https://quiltss.org/.)

As has been described, the learning journey in any TQI program or course is built out with the "end in mind." The backward design work that has occurred to this point, including identifying and defining competencies and determining how those competencies will be measured, will drive the creation of an intentionally designed learning journey. A helpful tool to begin intentionally designing the learning journey is a competency map. Competency maps for TQI include such components as competency area, definition, learning outcomes, summative assessment/workplace scenarios, required demonstration, learning module topics, and key learning content. The competency map communicates the design of the learning journey built to expected outcomes. (See https://quiltss.org/programs/.)

Learning must be scaffolded in such a way that each learner has foundational knowledge on which to build skills and abilities that lead to performance of the identified competency areas. TQI builds the learner's knowledge and skills in a systematic manner. This is done by benchmarking growth at key levels of learning, such as asking the learner to identify knowledge and skills, recognize the knowledge and skills in practice, and demonstrate the knowledge and skills in workplace-relevant situations. By following this *identify, recognize, demonstrate* sequence, TQI is able to scaffold learning in such a way that learners practice and gain the competencies needed for the workplace role. Consider the following example: First, the learner may be asked to identify the appropriate steps in a process. Perhaps this is accomplished through a formative learning activity that asks the learner to sequence the steps of the process. Second, the learner may be asked to recognize the appropriate steps of the process in practice. Perhaps this is accomplished through a video or observation of an authentic workplace situation in which the learner recognizes the appropriate steps of a given process in practice. Third, the learner may be asked to demonstrate the appropriate steps of the process in a relevant workplace situation. It is then essential that learners are able to demonstrate the process fluently, meaning with automaticity, as well as transfer such learning to the workplace.

In TQI programs, workplace practice activities are essential to creating new habits of behavior where they matter the most. Behavioral tools such as the "cue card" are used to transfer knowledge and skills into the workplace with discrete prompts (or cues) for behaviors that demonstrate the respective competency area. All behavioral tools are available for immediate use in the learning management system. See the following example (Figure 6.1) of the cue card for communication competency.

Figure 6.1. Cue card for communication competency.

I show **Communication** competency by doing the following:

- I use person-first language to put the person before the disability and diagnosis
- I keep personal information confidential
- I use common language and avoid using jargon, acronyms, abbreviations, and other specialized language with the person and their family
- I actively work to eliminate misunderstandings in my communication with others
- I practice active listening skills
- I monitor the speed, volume, and tone of my speech
- I provide accurate and clearly written documentation in progress notes, daily logs, charting, emails, etc.
- I recognize barriers and obstacles in my communication with others and make changes as needed

In order to achieve these benchmarks of successful progress, the learning content is designed to provide many safe practice opportunities across a range of assessment types. The variety of assessment types are carefully aligned with expectation of demonstration at that point in the learning journey. These assessment types include objective assessments, such as multiple choice or true/false, that measure knowledge acquisition. These build with level of learning to include assessment types, such as decision trees and video case studies, that measure recognition of expected performance in real-life situations. Ultimately these build with level of learning to include assessment types, such as workplace simulation exercises, that measure demonstration of expected performance in real-to-life situations.

A majority of the assessment types used as formative assessment—assessment *for* learning—that are sprinkled throughout the learning journey were accomplished through the creation of a variety of media items as well as behavioral-based tools that intentionally guide the learner from knowledge acquisition to knowledge application and finally to successful performance, supporting the transfer of learning into the workplace role. For example, over 500 custom media items have been created for TQI training programs, showing the institute's commitment to giving examples of authentic, real-to-life situations and providing robust practice opportunities with feedback. To keep learners engaged, we use a range of different types of media items, including live actor videos, animations, voiceover videos, whiteboard videos, audio items, narration videos, and practice activity videos.

When building a robust learning journey based on an identified set of competency areas, it is essential to ensure there is an infrastructure in place that supports the needs of your program design. Courses are offered asynchronously through a mobile-ready online delivery platform with available synchronous support. Although learners will progress at their own pace through each TQI competency course asynchronously, the institute knows synchronous moments must be built into the learning journey to ensure learner grit and completion. Typically, TQI provides coaches who are trained to support learners as they complete coursework, especially after each unit of study. Throughout the training, the learner is supported by faculty, coaches, and mentors. Academically qualified faculty substantively interact with learners to support their progress as they build their knowledge, skills, and intellectual behaviors in each competency area and translate learning into the workplace. In the workplace, field mentors, such as a supervisor, can provide meaningful feedback, answer questions, and debrief workplace practice activities. Additionally, a success coach monitors student progress through the learning activities and content, offering encouragement, suggestions for pacing, and wraparound student services as needed to promote successful progress through the content. Coaches are generally financially incentivized based on the number of learners they coach and successfully complete.

As described in Steps 3 through 5, TQI training offerings require demonstration of the knowledge, skills, and intellectual behaviors that define each competency area. Completion of the content through participation is not enough; demonstration in a real-to-life context is necessary. This begins with clear and consistent performance expectations with an opportunity for the learner to respond in an authentic workplace situation. By outlining performance expectations as an early step in the design process, you can create an intentional and explicit learning journey that appropriately sequences content in a way that scaffolds or builds to performance. Once the learner is ready to demonstrate performance of the competency area(s), they experience TQI's virtual assessment with real-time interaction in an authentic workplace situation recruited from the field and validated by nationally recognized subject matter experts.

When a learner successfully demonstrates the competency at the desired level of mastery, the individual will earn a microcredential in the form of a badge (see https://quiltss.org/programs/). This badge is available in both a virtual form as well as a physical metal pin. This is a physical manifestation, like a framed degree one might hang on an office wall, of what they know and can do. Learners can wear it on their lanyard or on their clothing to represent the competency area they have successfully demonstrated. It can also be a motivating factor for the learner to drive completion.

All badges are recorded in a registry system. The registry supports the microcredentialing system by creating a database to house the badges earned by the learners and making training portable. Also, it works as a validation system of the actual badge(s) earned and allows for the training and credential to follow the learner. This means that the learner's training and earned badges can be validated if they change roles or employers in LTSS, and the quality of such training is transparent. Systems can be created to allow employers to validate quality training for the learner (see Figure 6.2). TQI's registry system allows for employers and individuals in planning and human resource practices to access completion information at the badge level, and it is available by geographical area if desired.

All TQI trainings have been designed in such a manner that accredited institutions of higher education could license the content, offer the program, and grant college credit. Additionally, institutions that offer prior learning assessment credit could choose to accept QuILTSS badges for college credit. TQI training offerings are built using an accreditation-compliant curriculum design process and federal financial aid–complaint substantive

Figure 6.2. Registry system.

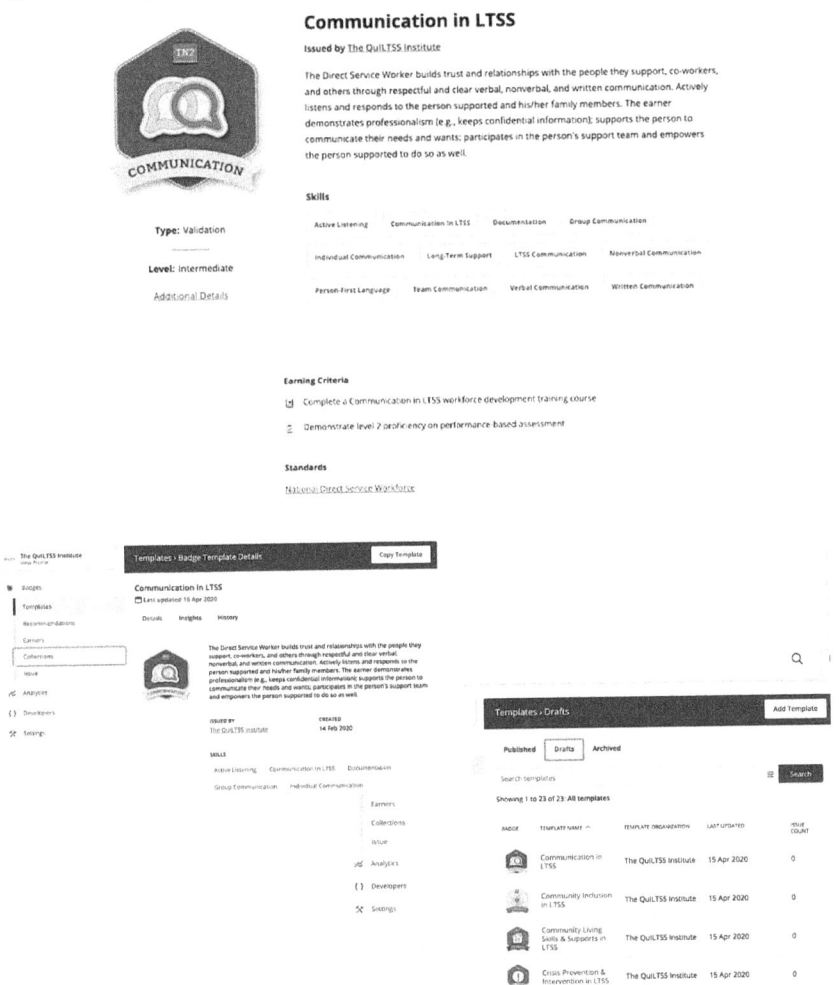

faculty interaction touchpoints. As described in Step 2, this is why the TBR has a master service agreement with TQI, so any of its community colleges and colleges of applied technology can license QuILTSS courses as part of their academic offerings. In Tennessee, the QuILTSS WFD training offering consists of 12 competency areas with each course equating to 1–2 hours of college-level credit, combining for a total of 18 credit hours and allowing the learner to earn a postsecondary certificate in LTSS.

Through TQI programs, the learner earns badges by demonstrating needed competencies. Several TQI programs weave together to create clear career pathways. See Figure 6.3 for one example of a career pathway in LTSS.

Figure 6.3. Employment support pathway.

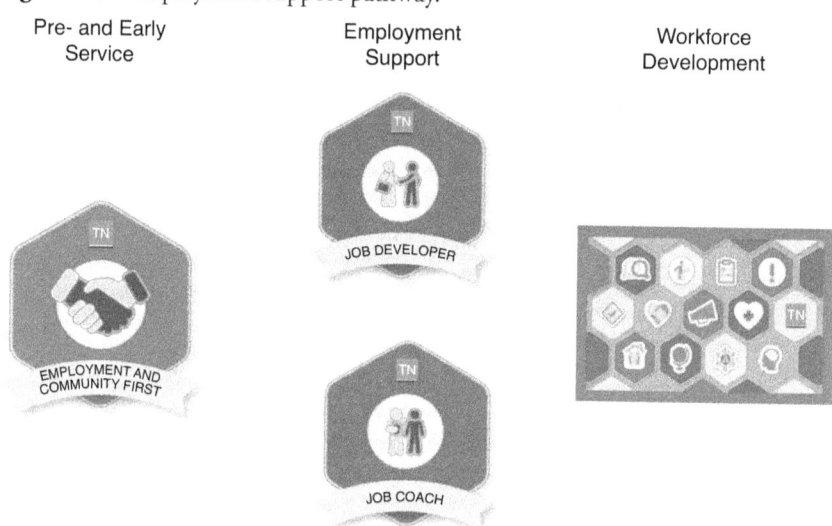

If states adopt a career pathway with alignment to the QuILTSS curriculum, this allows learners to see options for growth in their current role as well as moving into other more advanced roles. As described in Step 2, Tennessee is an example in which pay incentives for the individual worker are aligned with successful demonstration of competence in the 12 workforce development areas. For every four badges earned, a pay incentive of $0.50, $1.00, and $1.50, respectively, is provided. Once the full 12-course QuILTSS credential is earned, the pay incentives result in a total hourly increase of $3.00, equating to increased earnings of $6,000 per year for a full-time employee. An example of a Tennessee Career and Education Pathway can be found at https://quiltss.org/pathways/.

Points of Intersection: Illinois and Tennessee

Within the workforce context, program evaluation should comprise a macro-level representation of individual competencies. There is unlikely to be direct overlap in practitioner competencies and workplace program evaluation standards; however, each practitioner competency should logically fit within quality expectations communicated and assessed at the program level. For example, if workforce program requirements include maintaining a safe and healthy environment, competencies should clearly outline what employees should know and be able to do to attain and support that programmatic goal. Within the educational context, program evaluation should accurately reflect the composite of individual competency attainment and progression.

Academic program goals will be inclusive of competency attainment across individuals, and therefore attention needs to be paid to how to accurately measure competencies collectively. Within an academic course-based system, grade attainment, course completion, and retention are likely variables of measurement. Within a competency-based system, either comprised of individual competencies or competencies arranged in courses, variables of measurement might include such factors as the time needed to attain competency, retention across competencies, and overall progression.

Appendix 6A

 YOUR TURN

Adopting and implementing competencies into credentialing systems in educational and workforce contexts requires careful attention to logistical approvals and processes. Use the following table to apply information shared in this chapter to your own contexts.

TABLE 6.1
Adopting and Implementing Competencies in Your Credentialing System

Factor Influencing Competency Integration	Method of Data Collection/Analysis	Present Status	Trends Over Time	Goal
Use stakeholders to determine competency scope and impact.				
What is the influence of developed competencies on employers (e.g., is there clarity regarding how to support individuals in developing and refining essential proficiencies)?				
Are developed competencies relevant to workplace evaluation, mentorship, and continuous program evaluation?				

(Continues)

Table 6.1 (*Continued*)

Factor Influencing Competency Integration	Method of Data Collection/Analysis	Present Status	Trends Over Time	Goal
Are competency models transparent and easy to understand (e.g., supportive of progression, portable, and easily articulated)?				
What is the influence of developed competencies on educational institutions (e.g., is there clarity regarding how to support individuals in developing and refining essential proficiencies)?				
Are there clear pathways to developing and implementing systems at all levels on all students?				
Do competencies provide clarity and specificity in employment requirements?				
When used for performance evaluation, do competencies clearly and accurately reflect performance expectations?				
Do the competencies, as scaffolded, provide clear and accurate information regarding role progression?				
Is support for targeted competencies clearly reflected in the professional development system?				
Do professional development opportunities clearly and accurately support competency mastery and progression?				

Factor Influencing Competency Integration	Method of Data Collection/Analysis	Present Status	Trends Over Time	Goal
Do outlined competencies clearly and accurately complement expectations communicated through program evaluation?				
How do competencies impact the breadth of policies and processes in educational contexts?				
How do competencies impact the breadth of workplace policies and processes?				
Do developed competencies fully integrate into identified policies and processes?				
What tools (e.g., forms, policies, exemplars) do stakeholders need to fully support competency integration?				
What strategies should be used to develop and disseminate needed forms, policies, and exemplars?				

References

Alliance for Quality Career Pathways. (2014). *Shared vision, strong systems: The Alliance for Quality Career Pathways Framework version 1.0*. CLASP.

Book, P. A. (2014). *All hands on deck: Ten lessons from early adopters of competency-based education*. Western Interstate Commission for Higher Education. http://files.eric.ed.gov/fulltext/ED546830.pdf

Gateways to Opportunity. (n.d.). *ECE toolbox*. https://www.ilgateways.com/professional-development/higher-education-programs/ece-toolbox

Illinois Network of Child Care Resource and Referral Agencies. (2014). *Facts about the early care and education workforce in Illinois*. Gateways to Opportunity Illinois Professional Development System.

Klein-Collins, R. (2013, November). *Sharpening our focus on learning: The rise of competency-based approaches to degree completion.* National Institute for Learning Outcomes Assessment.

Phillips, K., & Schneider, C. (2016). *Policy, pilots, and the path to competency-based education: A tale of three states.* ExcelinEd. https://www.excelined.org/wp-content/uploads/2017/11/ExcelinEd.Policy.PilotsAndThePathToCBETaleOfThreeStates.Sep2016.pdf

Sanden, S., Darragh Ernst, J. C., Hamann, K., Quesenberry, A., Latham, N. I., Christianson, D., & Smyrniotis, A. (2016). Supporting early childhood workforce development and pathways: Developing a competency-based assessment system in Illinois. In S. A. Bernoteit, J. C. Darragh Ernst, & N. I. Latham (Eds.), *Voices from the field: Collaborative innovations in early childhood educator preparation* (pp. 200–223). Illinois Education Research Council; Illinois Board of Higher Education.

Smither, C., Parsons, K., Peek, A., & Soldner, M. (2016, August). *Key characteristics of postsecondary competency-based education programs: A descriptive rubric.* American Institutes for Research. http://www.air.org/sites/default/files/downloads/report/Descriptive%20CBE%20Rubric%20v20160819.pdf

Step 7

EVALUATING THE IMPACT OF COMPETENCIES OVER TIME AND SUPPORTING COMPETENCY SUSTAINABILITY

 Central Question: So, what? Did competencies make a difference?

Step 7 in our CDPM will take us all the way back to Step 1. An essential and often overlooked step in the competency design process is to think about how competency use and implementation across the professional spectrum will be evaluated and systematically examined for relevance and currency in shifting contexts and effectiveness in use. Evaluation of when and how competencies are used to inform and improve practice will systematically serve to strengthen the competencies and infuse them into professional practice in long-term, sustainable ways.

It is important to identify and keep central to the evaluation process what we refer to here as evaluation "touchpoints." These touchpoints are found in each of Steps 1–6 of the CDPM. The obvious evaluation process would be focused on a periodic review of the performance indicators and any necessary updating or revision. However, just as each step in the CDPM built on the previous step and informed the next step, the same is true for the evaluation process. Each individual step of the model should inform your substantive, continuous review process, which will in turn inform competency implementation, use, and revision.

In Step 1, workforce pathway challenges were identified that competencies could serve to mitigate or address. It can be assumed that these workforce challenges will change over time, especially as competencies are implemented and the identified pathway challenges are reduced or removed. However, the examination of previously identified workforce pathway and emerging issues should be a springboard for the evaluation process. Once these challenges are identified and there is opportunity for the assumed impact competencies were projected to have on these issues to occur, evaluation data on the success of these outcomes can be collected and the impact measured. This should include the stakeholder subgroups impacted by the identified challenges (preservice practitioners, in-service practitioners, preparation programs, field leadership, and state and national legislative leaders). These professionals can inform the identified issue not only from varied professional perspectives, but also across the professional practice spectrum.

Using the professional practitioner and expert groups identified in Step 1, and subsequently in Step 7, you can proceed to the next touchpoint, which is an examination of the competency framework developed in Step 2. It is important to systematically collect data to ascertain if the framework continues to undergird the competencies as professional demands, mandates, and expectations have shifted. Additionally, the competency framework should be updated as needed to reflect changing professional standards.

An obvious point in the evaluation process focuses on the performance indicators themselves. It is important to develop a systematic process for reviewing performance indicators over time as well as establish processes for how sequencing and leveling of the performance indicators will be reviewed through the lens of shifting professional mandates, requirements, expectations, and standards. Two more evaluation points to consider and include in the process are making sure that the developed scoring tools and the assessment tasks are authentically measuring the performance indicator(s) they claim to measure and providing data to inform and enhance professional practice. Evaluating the scoring tools should also include review for usability, reliability (including inter-rater) and validity. Lastly, the processes, procedures, and policies based on the competencies should also be examined as part of a thorough evaluation system. Including these identified processes and systems in Step 6 will consistently identify possible system or implementation issues that could be hindering the full realization of competencies on professional practice.

For each previously identified evaluation touchpoint, specific evaluation questions should be determined. From those questions, specific data to help inform or better understand each question should also be developed. Thinking about these data and data sources should include the different stakeholder groups applicable (preservice practitioners, in-service practitioners, preparation programs, evaluation of practice in the field, and leadership) and the varying levels (institutional, employer, individual versus state, national, local, etc.) representing the professional practice spectrum. The evaluation plan should also use the formal and informal contexts identified in Step 2 to establish control variables or a lens through which you can analyze your evaluation data. Lastly, your evaluation system needs to consider how data will physically or electronically be collected and maintained in a consistent, valid way over time. These considerations should include protection of identifiable data if applicable, along with how data requests will be made in secure environments to protect data transfer. Key decisions will also need to be made about which parties will be responsible for systematic data collection at different levels. For example, determinations should be made about the responsibilities of higher education programs, professional development system providers, and state agencies carrying out this work. As part of your evaluation plan, it is also important to consider how data will be analyzed in relation to your evaluation questions. Thinking about and planning for analysis will help solidify what data are collected. Considering analyses will specifically help in making sure information is collected and linked, which will allow for patterns and trends to be identified while controlling for variables that inform those trends and patterns.

 **Remodeling the House: The Illinois ECE Story**

The development and use of competencies in Illinois is still a work in progress, and competencies continue to be implemented and embedded at deeper and deeper levels in our Illinois credentialing systems. During the creation of our competencies, we strove to and continue to consider the evaluation uses of competencies to inform program design and quality across the broad spectrum of ECE teacher preparation programs in the state. Since the competency model in Illinois is still being embedded, the longitudinal goals of our evaluation system continue to come to fruition.

It is the intent of our model that as the ECE competency system is completely embedded in all preparation programs and systematic annual data collection completed, analysis of these data can help us better understand program quality and direction over time. We specifically designed our evaluation elements to allow preparation program experts at all levels (2-year programs, 4-year programs, and graduate-level programs) to design their own assessment experiences and tasks while using the established scoring tools. This will provide longitudinal data which can be disaggregated by program type, program size, program participant demographics, ECE credential area, and geographic location. Table 7.1 is an example of how cumulative data could be collected from the scoring tools designed and analyzed over time. These analysis opportunities can inform not only quality program design but also our understanding of equity and access issues.

As discussed earlier, "toolboxes" have been created to provide sample assessment tasks for programs to use in collecting their program evaluation data. In addition, scoring tools include supportive documents to aggregate evaluation data across semesters and/or cohorts as well as to use in accreditation and credential agency reporting. These supports also allow for the evaluation tools to be used for in-service professional development data collection as well. Table 7.1 is also an example of data collection/analysis that provides professional standards alignment with the performance indicators so that these data can also be used for professional accreditation and state licensure reporting. We are looking forward in Illinois to the long-term analysis of the evaluation data generated from our competency model and using it to inform program development and improvement over time.

TABLE 7.1
Health, Safety, and Well-Being Competency Area
Cumulative Evaluation Data Table

Competency and Standards Alignment					Cumulative Assessment Data				
Competency	NAEYC Stand. (Draft 2020) 6b	NAEYC Comp. (Draft 2020)	IPTS (2013) 4G	InTASC (2019)	Distinguished	Proficient	Needs Improvement	Unsatisfactory	Unable to Assess
ECE HSW1: Articulates components of a safe and healthy environment	6b	6b-LVL1-3-4	4G	3(k)					
ECE HSW2: Maintains a safe and healthy environment	1d, 6b	1d-LVLI-2, 6b-LVLI-3	4I	3(k)					

Building From a Blueprint: The Tennessee LTSS Story

As described in Step 1, The Bureau of TennCare contracted with National Research Corporation (NRC) Health in early 2019 to conduct an initial satisfaction and cultural change survey, where 100% of the state's 286 Medicaid facilities participated. The data was aggregated statewide and also provided key strengths and opportunities of each nursing facility. NRC Health provided comparisons to statewide and national benchmarks. The results clearly demonstrated the need to enhance the knowledge, skills, abilities, and intellectual behaviors of frontline DSWs in the field of LTSS to deliver higher quality, more person-centered care. To achieve this, a recommendation was issued to develop competencies beyond what is required for licensure in applicable job roles, with higher quality training and increased competency in areas identified by staff and residents. As you can see, evaluation is where this project began, and it drove the development of this model.

A second significant evaluation touchpoint includes the implementation of a value-based purchasing model for nursing facility (NF) payment reimbursement (see Figure 7.1). This model incentivizes NFs to meet clearly articulated quality dimensions in order to receive an increased payment based on their performance. Staff training is one of the measures for which NFs may be incentivized. Although all quality dimensions are impacted by

Figure 7.1. QuILTSS quality framework.

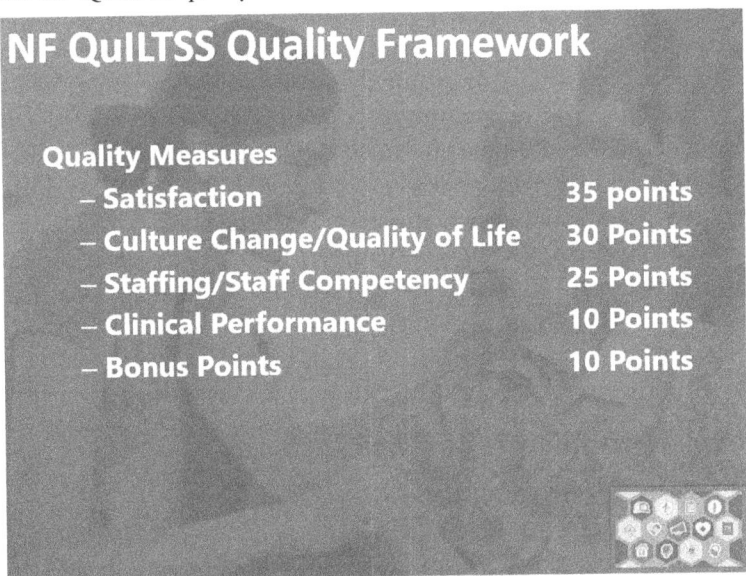

the overall competence of the staff, 5% of the reimbursement model is based solely on the staff training measure.

Under TennCare's QuILTSS initiative, NF payment is based in part on residents' assessed levels of need and is adjusted based on quality metrics. Providers are rewarded with higher reimbursement payments when they improve the member's experience of care and promote a person-centered care delivery model. For these reasons, the evaluation of competencies and their implementation in the training of frontline DSWs providing services and supports for older adults is essential. One way to do this—and a third evaluation touchpoint—is the collection and use of data related to improved quality of care and life as perceived by those receiving long-term services and supports and their families. In order to collect such data, TennCare and TQI contracted with NRC Health to conduct annual satisfaction and cultural change surveys. There are Resident, Family, and Staff Satisfaction Survey instruments. TennCare shares the aggregate results of this survey with the Department of Health and CMS to contribute to and inform future regulatory or funding priorities.

In addition to the annual NRC Health surveys, a fourth evaluation touchpoint includes competency course evaluations offered to all learners at the conclusion of each competency course, and an overall program evaluation after completion of their final summative assessment. This evaluation solicits feedback on a range of topics including instructor and success coach professionalism and performance, course rigor and relevance, and the quality and immediate applicability of the competency content in the work environment. A fifth evaluation touchpoint includes the use of formative assessments and activities conducted during each course. These formative activities solicit feedback on how newly acquired knowledge, skills, abilities, and intellectual behaviors are leading to improved resident outcomes. These activities and assessments include opportunities for DSWs to practice their competencies and to teach peers new strategies too. These evaluations are summarized annually for trends and shared quarterly with stakeholders. The resulting feedback is considered in modifying competency courses and the administration of the program. All data are shared with the Tennessee Department of Health and the CMS regularly.

Points of Intersection: Illinois and Tennessee

An evaluation plan is basically meaningless if the findings are not systematically reviewed, used, and disseminated. Expectation and planning for this review, use, and dissemination should intentionally include stakeholder groups connected to Steps 1 through 6. The use of findings across the profession should inform professional preparation, professional development in the field, evaluation of professional practice, field leadership, state and national legislative mandates, and decision-making, funding, and policy. Decisions you made earlier about the responsibilities assumed by higher education programs, professional development system providers, and state agencies will also inform the roles of these same entities in reviewing, disseminating, and using findings.

Appendix 7A

 YOUR TURN

The following questions will guide your thinking as you consider what your evaluation plan will look like. Although performance indicators are final at this point, it is possible that considering how you evaluate competency effectiveness and use those findings could lead to reconsidering or refining your assessments and system implementation. The following information will help you as you build your evaluation plan.

Workforce Pathway Challenges

1. List your identified workforce pathway challenges from Step 1 and the anticipated goal/impact of competencies on each identified challenge.

TABLE 7.2
Goal/Outcome of Competencies on Workforce Challenges

Workforce Pathway Challenge/Issue (From Step 1)	*The Anticipated Goal or Outcome Resulting From Using Competencies to Impact This Challenge*

2. How have stakeholder groups impacted by the identified challenges implemented competencies to mitigate these challenges (preservice practitioners, in-service practitioners, preparation programs, evaluation of practice in the field, field leadership, and state and national legislative leaders)?

The Competency Framework

3. How is the framework continually reviewed to undergird the competencies as professional demands, mandates, and expectations shift?
4. How is professional standard alignment systematically updated and verified with content experts?

The Performance Indicators

5. How will the performance indicators be reviewed over time?
   5a. What will the review criteria be?
   5b. What will the review process and timing look like?
6. How will sequencing and leveling of the performance indicators be reviewed through the previous process? How will shifting professional mandates (standards and requirements) be considered?

Competency Scoring Tools

7. How will the periodic review of performance indicators include the review and revision of the corresponding scoring tools?
8. How will scoring tools be reviewed for usability, reliability (including inter-rater) and validity? Establish criteria for each.
   8a. Usability
   8b. Reliability
   8c. Validity

Assessment Tasks

9. How will the periodic review of performance indicators and scoring tools include the review and revision of the corresponding assessment tasks?

Competency Integration and Use Across Systems

10. How will systems impacted by competencies be reviewed and evaluated?
11. How will logistical and procedural barriers to substantive use be identified?

Data Collection

12. What specific data will need to be collected:
    12a. for different stakeholder groups if applicable (preservice practitioners, in-service practitioners, preparation programs, evaluation of practice in the field, leadership)?
    12b. at varying levels (institutional, employer, individual versus state, national, local, etc.)?
13. What data will be used to establish control variables or lenses through which you can analyze your evaluation data (some of these can be determined from the formal and informal contexts identified in Step 2)?
14. How will data be collected and maintained in a safe, consistent, valid way over time?
    14a. How will data be requested?
    14b. How will data be securely transferred?
    14c. How will data be securely maintained?

Data Analysis

15. How will data be analyzed to best understand impact?
16. How will analysis flexibly handle shifting mandates, expectations, and trends in the field?

Reviewing, Disseminating, and Using Findings for Program Improvement and Field Growth

1. How will findings be articulated to varying stakeholders?
2. How will findings be disseminated to stakeholders?
3. Who should the communication network, representative of the identified experts in Steps 1–6, consist of?
4. What are expectations for data use by individual stakeholders?

5. How will data informed practice be encouraged in regard to professional preparation programs, professional development in the field, evaluation of practice in the field, field leadership, state and national legislative mandates and decision-making, funding, and policy?

CONCLUSION

The CDPM explicated in the previous chapters draws from fundamental elements of career pathway and competency-based education program design. This is coupled with the authors' perspectives regarding what is typically given insufficient treatment in the professional literature about the fundamental interdependence of competencies and assessments. Competency development processes must, from the viewpoint and experience of the authors, contain iterative processes that test and refine competency areas against the practical matters of assessment and broader professional systems integration. Our CDPM provides a clear "how-to" process for those interested in developing the foundational expressions of knowledge, skills, and intellectual behaviors—competencies—that undergird CBE/CBL programs. C-BEN (2017) has defined this step of creating "clear, measurable, meaningful, and integrated competencies" as a key feature of its "Quality Framework for Competency-Based Education Programs" (p. 4).

The CDPM also makes transparent a series of practical and iterative steps for designing competencies that also intentionally support program evaluation, professional credentialing, performance evaluation, and ongoing workforce development systems.

The CDPM has value and utility in both higher education and the workforce when actively engaged in the design and implementation of CBE programs as well as CBL approaches within more traditional programs. The CDPM also has practical application regardless of whether the higher education program is engaged in career pathway design work or vice versa. The exercise of thoughtfully delineating learner expectations through the lens of competencies and determining how evidence of learner demonstration of these expectations will be both measured and documented as evidence is valuable for a number of reasons. Those who use the CDPM will bring greater coherence and clarity to program and competency design efforts internal to their own organizations. The resulting competencies, and the collaborative processes described in the CDPM for creating them, bring opportunities for professional development and evidence-based program improvement. Perhaps most importantly, the CDPM creates opportunities for programs to help learners more clearly understand what they will know and be able to do, how they are making progress toward competence, and what the measures of competency attainment look like. Learners will also be empowered to communicate to potential employers the key transferrable competencies they possess and provide compelling examples of their ability to demonstrate the same.

In our stories, the authors have continued to consider the CDPM in light of current, emerging, and visionary conditions relative to the fields of ECE and LTSS. The robust competencies resulting from our practical applications of the CDPM have permitted us to subject the field-based competencies to several rigorous tests of applicability to particular focus areas of practice. This also means the CDPM has served us well in the design of new credentials in each field. For early childhood educators in bilingual/ESL, one specifically designed credential bridges the needs of the professionals in the state's licensed child-care settings with a credential currently available for K–12 educators. For long-term care workers, the credentials are specifically designed as currency in the workforce, leading to higher pay and portability of training, as well as currency in higher education, offering transcription for college-level credit. In both situations, the time and effort involved in creating competencies and considering related systems through the CDPM has afforded our states the opportunity to effectively move forward in matters of strategic importance for our states' most vulnerable populations and their families.

Clear, measurable, meaningful, and integrated competencies (C-BEN, 2017) are the bedrock of CBE/CBL programs. They also provide the foundation for an exciting future envisioned by many in higher education, industry, and technology fields—a future in which competencies become the currency of learning and can be meaningfully understood, evidenced, and used by a wide variety of stakeholders. The authors trust the CDPM offers a small contribution to this larger vision.

Reference

Competency-Based Education Network. (2017). *Quality framework for competency-based education programs.* https://www.cbenetwork.org/wp-content/uploads/2018/09/1st_button_CBE17016__Quality_Framework_Update.pdf

ABOUT THE AUTHORS

Nancy I. Latham currently serves as the associate dean for the College of Education and executive director of the Council of Teacher Education and a research associate professor in the Curriculum and Instruction Department at the University of Illinois at Urbana-Champaign (UIUC). For the past 10 years she has served as a lead consultant on statewide early childhood employment pathway efforts in Illinois and teacher preparation pathway competency development and implementation. Latham has published and presented extensively on teacher attrition, specifically the impacts of teacher preparation models on teacher persistence in the field, and coauthored and edited *Voices From the Field: Collaborative Innovations in Early Childhood Educator Preparation* (Bernoteit et al., Illinois Education Research Council, 2016), which overviews the statewide experience of competency implementation for early childhood credentialing in Illinois.

Prior to joining UIUC she served as an administrator and early childhood professor at Illinois State University. In addition, she was a tenured community college professor and a public-school teacher and administrator. Her external leadership has included serving as president of the Illinois Association of Early Childhood Teacher Education and representing the Illinois public university colleges of education on the Illinois State Educator Professional Licensure Board. She recently led an Illinois State Board of Education project to revise the state teaching standards to a competency-based system. Her research interests focus on teacher employment pathways and trends, teacher persistence in the field, and the impacts of teacher preparation models and practices on teacher retention and attrition.

Johnna Darragh Ernst is a distinguished professor of ECE at Heartland Community College in Normal, Illinois and the project director of Competency-Based Education Pathways. For the past several years, her work has focused on collaboratively developing competency-based pathways supporting early childhood practitioners in Illinois and serving as a lead consultant in developing the Illinois ECE Competency-Based Assessment System. Together with Nancy Latham, Darragh Ernst coordinated the movement of seven Illinois credentials to a competency-based system. Her work includes supporting the modularization and implementation of several credentials across Illinois higher education institutions and within Heartland. In addition to publishing numerous articles, she has authored two early childhood textbooks focusing on inclusion and family engagement. She coauthored and edited *Voices From the Field: Collaborative Innovations in Early Childhood Educator Preparation* (Bernoteit et al., Illinois Education Research Council, 2016), which focuses on the Illinois effort to develop a competency-based model of early childhood educator preparation.

Her current external leadership relating to CBE includes serving as a tri-chair on the Illinois Professional Development Advisory Council and as a member of the Illinois State Competency Leadership Team. She is on the steering committee for the Illinois State Board of Education's project, which serves to move state teaching standards to competencies. She has also worked to support the development and implementation of Walden University's innovative Tempo Learning CBE program. Within Heartland, Darragh Ernst has created several CBL pathways designed to maximize student access, decrease student cost, and minimize time to credential and degree.

Tiffany Freeze has extensive experience building CBE programs in higher education and work-based settings. She currently serves as the chief assessment officer of TQI in which she leads the design and build of CBE programs. Additionally, she serves as a principal consultant with C-BEN, working with institutions nationwide to design CBE programs. She is an experienced and credentialed leader of assessment centers and virtually delivered behavior-based assessment using the latest technologies. Freeze codirected C-BEN's Competency-Based Assessment Collaboratory project, in partnership with 20+ institutional leaders, to release new assessment resources to the field in 2021. Freeze also served as the 2020 president for the Tennessee Association for Behavior Analysis. In this role, Freeze led the organization alongside the executive committee to hold regional and state-level meetings, advocate for members, provide workshops, inform legislation, among other priorities in the field of applied behavior analysis.

Prior to her current role, Freeze served as assistant dean in the College of Professional Studies at Lipscomb University where she led the Curriculum and Academic Team to the launch of PACE, Lipscomb's 126-credit hour competency-based program. She also served as an assistant professor, administrator of Lipscomb's CORE Assessment Center, and engaged multiple employer partnerships. She spent 6 years studying at The University of Memphis earning the master of arts and education specialist degrees in school psychology, and the doctor of education degree in applied behavior analysis. She is recognized as a nationally certified school psychologist and board-certified behavior analyst with doctoral designation.

Stephanie Bernoteit serves as executive deputy director at the Illinois Board of Higher Education (IBHE). She oversees the agency's regulatory and consumer protection work with approximately 450 postsecondary institutions and is responsible for the agency's initiatives to promote postsecondary student success. Stephanie collaboratively leads a statewide effort to enact a competency-based system of educator preparation, professional development, and credentialing in the field of ECE in Illinois. She is coauthor and editor of publications on the subject including *Advancing the Illinois Early Childhood Education Workforce: A Model College and Career Pathway* (Bernoteit et al., Illinois Education Research Council, 2017) and *Voices From the Field: Collaborative Innovations in Early Childhood Educator Preparation* (Bernoteit et al., Illinois Education Research Council, 2016). Bernoteit serves on the board of directors of C-BEN and is a member of the Executive Committee of the Illinois Early Learning Council.

Prior to joining the IBHE, Bernoteit worked at Illinois State University as executive director for alumni relations and codirector of the School of Education's National Board Resource Center. A national board certified teacher in early childhood from 1996–2016, Stephanie spent several years at the National Board for Professional Teaching Standards to higher education to advance board certification for educators across the United States. She also worked as an early childhood and elementary classroom teacher in the West Des Moines Community School District. Stephanie holds a doctorate in education from Illinois State University, a graduate certificate in nonprofit leadership from Georgetown University, a master's degree in education from Drake University, and a bachelor's degree in elementary education with an emphasis in early childhood from Northwest Missouri State University.

Bradford R. White is an education researcher who studies workforce development and human resources management issues throughout the P–20 spectrum. His work focuses on state-level education policy issues and educator preparation and evaluation. From 2004 through 2018, Brad was part of the Illinois Education Research Council (IERC) at Southern Illinois University Edwardsville, which served as the research arm of the state's education agencies. At the IERC, he led an evaluation of the Illinois Board of Higher Education's Early Childhood Educator Preparation Program Innovation grants, as well as studies of the state's teacher and principal workforces. He also served on the Illinois State Board of Education's Partnership for Educator Preparation, the Illinois Education and Workforce Data Task Group, the Illinois Longitudinal Data System Data Advisory Committee, and the Teacher and Leader Excellence Committee of the Illinois P–20 Council. He is currently a data analyst in the Office of Institutional Research at Lewis & Clark Community College in Godfrey, Illinois.

INDEX

accountability, 3, 31, 106
adopt and implement competencies in learning journey and credentialing system step
   within Building From a Blueprint (Tennessee LTSS Story), 111–116
   educational institutions within, 107–108
   employer role within, 106
   overview of, 105–106
   pre- and in-service professionals within, 107
   within Remodeling the House (Illinois ECE Story), 108–111
   table for, 117–119
adult learners, meeting demands of, 3–5
affordability, importance of, 4–5
Alliance for Quality Career Pathways, 108
Assessment Outline, 80
assessment/assessment experience
   behaviorally based, 99–102
   of career pathways, 38-39
   for competencies, 19–20, 88
   for Cultural Competency (Building From a Blueprint), 100
   determination need within, 88
   formative, 100, 113
   of Health, Safety, and Wellness (HSW), 92–97
   leveling of, 91
   piloting of, 103
   review of, 89
   scoring tool matching within, 89
   simulation scenarios for, 100–101, 103
   stakeholder involvement regarding, 102–103
   structuring or packaging within, 89
   summative, 100
   vetting of, 102–103
   workshopping of, 103
assessors, role of, 79

backward design
   within Building From a Blueprint (Tennessee LTSS Story), 111
   of competency-based programs, 7, 10, 28, 29, 56
   example of, 80
   learning journey within, 105, 110
   stages of, 17–19
badges, from TQI (QuILTSS Institute), 110, 111, 114, 115–116
behavior, 80, 81
behavioral hits, 102
behavioral science, 71
benchmarks, professional, 57–58, 59–60
Building From a Blueprint (Tennessee LTSS Story)
   adopt and implement competencies in learning journey and credentialing system step within, 111–116
   assessing competency framework fit within, 63
   assessor role within, 79
   competency areas within, 102
   competency course evaluation within, 126
   constituent feedback within, 63–65

INDEX

core curriculum committees (CCCs) within, 62
cue card within, 112
define the pathway problem step within, 32–38
develop competency assessment step within, 99–103
draft competency statements step within, 62–65
drafting representative performance indicators within, 62
establish competency measurability step within, 78–82
establish the competency framework step within, 49–53
evaluating the impact of competencies over time and supporting competency sustainability step within, 125–126
incentivization requirements within, 125–126
person-centered practices within, 64
rating scale within, 81
scoring tools within, 79–82
Stakeholder Advisory Group within, 63
statement vetting within, 63–65
Bureau of TennCare (Tennessee), 33–38, 63, 125–126. *See also* Building From a Blueprint (Tennessee LTSS Story)

career pathways/career pathways approach
assessment of, 38–39
competencies arranged in, 107
competency-based system based on, 106
links within, 26
overview of, 13–16
questions regarding, 39
of Remodeling the House (Illinois ECE Story), 30, 47, 108
steps within, 16
within TQI (QuILTSS Institute), 115–116
See also define the pathway problem step
career performance, challenges of, 42
career preparation, challenges and factors of, 27–28, 42, 43
coaches, within TQI (QuILTSS Institute), 113
communication competency, 51, 112
Communication competency area (Building From a Blueprint), 102
communication, clarity within, 107
comparability, importance of, 3
competencies
adopting and implementing, 117–119
assessment for, 19–20, 88
within career pathways approach, 14, 107
defined, 17
for employment roles, 17
evaluation of, 21, 121–123
evidence of, 20
graphic representation of, 18, 19
integration of, 107–108, 109
for intrainstitutional articulation, 32
performance of, 20–21
professional development and, 109
as a tool, 31–32
utilization of, 107
See also evaluating the impact of competencies over time and supporting competency sustainability step
competency area framework, 59–60, 63, 66–67
Competency Assessment Guide (Remodeling the House), 110
competency course, evaluation of, 126
competency development process model (CDPM), 12–21, 106, 109, 131–132

INDEX   *139*

See also Building From a Blueprint (Tennessee LTSS Story); Remodeling the House (Illinois ECE Story); *specific steps*
competency development, framework origin approach for, 44
competency mapping process, 107
competency performance indicators, 26
competency statements step, draft
  assessing competency framework fit within, 59–60, 63
  within Building From a Blueprint (Tennessee LTSS Story), 62–65
  drafting representative performance indicators within, 58–59, 62
  overview of, 56–57
  within Remodeling the House (Illinois ECE Story), 57–62
  statement vetting within, 60–62, 63–65
competency-based education (CBE)
  affordability of, 4–5
  agnostic regarding learning source within, 10
  design examples of, 12–21
  examples of, 7
  features of, 9–11
  flexibility of, 4
  intentional backward design of, 10
  modularization within, 11
  outcomes emphasis within, 10
  overview of, 1, 6–11
  pedagogical motivations regarding, 1–2
  personalization within, 11
  quality assurance within, 2–3
  rigorous requirements within, 10–11
  students at the center within, 11
  transparency within, 11
competency-based learning (CBL), 6–7
competency-based programs, backward design of, 28
Connecting Credentials project, 5

constituents, feedback from, 60–62, 63–65
content analysis, 49
core curriculum committees (CCCs), 62
credit hour model, requirements for, 20
cue card, 112
Cultural Competency (Building From a Blueprint), 100
curriculum, workforce requirements and, 16

deconstruction-reconstruction approach, 44, 46–47, 108
define the pathway problem step
  within Building From a Blueprint (Tennessee), 32–38
  overview of, 14–16, 26–27
  questions regarding, 38–39
  recruiting and preparation challenges within, 27–28
  within Remodeling the House (Illinois), 29–32
  training and, 35–38
  workforce participation, performance, and persistence challenges within, 28–29
develop competency assessment step
  assessment experience review within, 89
  within Building From a Blueprint (Tennessee LTSS Story), 99–103
  creating assessment experiences that produce measurable evidence within, 88–89
  determine assessment experiences needed within, 88
  matching scoring tools to assessment experiences within, 89
  overview of, 87–88
  within Remodeling the House (Illinois ECE Story), 90–99
  simulation scenarios within, 100–101

structuring or packaging assessment experiences based on field expectations within, 89
direct assessment programs, within competency-based education (CBE), 7–8
direct pathway (Remodeling the House), 108
direct service workers (DSWs), 33, 49–50, 99, 125. *See also* Building From a Blueprint (Tennessee LTSS Story)
draft competency statements step
  assessing competency framework fit within, 59–60, 63
  within Building From a Blueprint (Tennessee LTSS Story), 62–65
  drafting representative performance indicators within, 58–59, 62
  overview of, 56–57
  within Remodeling the House (Illinois ECE Story), 57–62
  statement vetting within, 60–62, 63–65
Drive to 55, 53

early childhood education (ECE)
  educational pathway for, 30
  educational roles within, 30
  Human Growth and Development (HGD) assessment, 61
  settings regarding, 45
  statistics regarding, 30
  See also Remodeling the House (Illinois ECE Story)
educational institutions, within adopt and implement competencies in learning journey and credentialing system step, 107–108
employers
  within adopt and implement competencies in learning journey and credentialing system step, 106
  as coleaders and coinvestors, 14–15
entitled pathway (Remodeling the House), 108

establish competency measurability step
  analyzing indicator verbs for measurability within, 70
  within Building From a Blueprint (Tennessee LTSS Story), 78–82
  building performance criteria within, 71
  developing performance scoring tools within, 71
  overview of, 69–70
  performance criteria and scoring tool review within, 72
  within Remodeling the House (Illinois ECE story), 72–78
establish the competency framework step
  Building From a Blueprint (Tennessee LTSS Story) and, 49–53
  overview of, 42–45
  Remodeling the House (Illinois ECE Story) and, 45–49
evaluating the impact of competencies over time and supporting competency sustainability step
  within Building From a Blueprint (Tennessee LTSS Story), 125–126
  overview of, 121–123
  plan formation process within, 127–130
  within Remodeling the House (Illinois ECE Story), 123–124

families and communities (FCR), performance indicators for, 90–91
feedback, 35–37, 60–62, 63–65, 72
field expectations, assessment experience structuring based on, 89
Final Competency Set for the Direct Service Workforce (Building From a Blueprint), 50–51
flexibility, 4
formal expectations, 43
formative assessment, 100, 113. *See also* assessment
framework origin approach, for competency development, 44

Gateways to Opportunity ECE Credentials system
  benchmark reorganization within, 47–49
  characteristics of, 110
  overview of, 30–31, 46
  pathways for, 108
  toolbox within, 109–110, 124
  See also Remodeling the House (Illinois ECE Story)

Haslam, Bill, 53
Health, Safety, and Wellness (HSW) (Remodeling the House), 91, 92–97, 98, 124
Human Growth and Development (HGD) (Remodeling the House), 58–59, 61, 72
hybrid programs, characteristics of, 8

identify, recognize, demonstrate sequence (TQI), 112
Illinois Professional Teaching Standards, 46
incentivization, requirements for, 125–126
indicator verbs, 70, 72–73, 79, 82–83
Interactions, Relationships, and Environments (IRE) (Remodeling the House), 73–78

knowledge, within developmental progression, 48

learning journey
  backward design and, 18–19
  within Building From a Blueprint (Tennessee LTSS Story), 113
  construction of, 105
  personalization within, 11
  within Remodeling the House (Illinois ECE Story), 110–111
  student/practitioner skill development within, 106
  See also adopt and implement competencies in learning journey and credentialing system step
leveling
  of assessment experiences, 91
  of Building From a Blueprint (Tennessee LTSS Story), 54
  defined, 47
  example of, 48
  of Remodeling the House (Illinois ECE Story), 54
  of TQI (QuILTSS Institute), 53
  understanding and visualizing of, 91
levels of employment, 43
Lipscomb University, 34
listening behavior, 18
listening intent/potential, 18
long-term services and supports (LTSS) (Building From a Blueprint), 32–38. *See also* Building From a Blueprint (Tennessee LTSS Story)

mastery learning pedagogy, 2
measurability, 69–70, 88–89
modularization, 20–21

NAEYC Standards for Professional Preparation, 46
National Direct Service Workforce Resource Center (DSW RC), 50
National Research Corporation (NRC) Health, 125
non-direct assessment programs, within competency-based education (CBE), 8
nontraditional students, meeting demands of, 3–5
nursing facility (NF), 125–126
nursing, educational and workforce contexts within, 44

observable behavior, 71
Observation and Assessment competency area, indicator verbs within, 72–73

open classroom movement, 1–2
overt behavior, 71

pacing, 20–21
participation, workforce, 28–29
performance criteria
  building, 71
  creating higher level, 84
  creating lower level, 83
  Interactions, Relationships, and Environments (IRE) within, 74–78
  scoring tool review and, 72
performance indicators
  analyzing, 82–83
  within Building From a Blueprint (Tennessee LTSS Story), 78–79
  building performance criteria for, 71
  development of, 103
  evaluation step and, 122
  of families and communities (FCR), 90–91
  function of, 108
  for Health, Safety, and Wellness, 91
  holistic impact of, 105–106
  of Interactions, Relationships, and Environments (IRE), 73–78
  measurability of, 69–70
  within Observation and Assessment competency area, 72–73
  scoring tools for, 71
  verbs for, 70, 72–73, 79, 82–83
performance, workforce, 28–29, 43
persistence, workforce, 28–29
person-centered practices (Building From a Blueprint), 64
Personalized System of Instruction, 2
portability, 3, 31
pre- and in-service professionals, within adopt and implement competencies in learning journey and credentialing system step, 107
preparation pathways, challenges of, 27–28
primary content set, 44–45

primary standard set, 44–45
professional benchmarks, 57–58, 59–60
professional development, 26–27, 109

Quality Improvement in Long-Term Services and Supports Workforce Development (QuILTSS WFD) Initiative, 32–38, 52–53, 111, 115, 125. *See also* Building From a Blueprint (Tennessee LTSS Story)
QuILTSS Institute (TQI). *See* TQI (QuILTSS Institute)

rating scale, 81
recruiting, challenges of, 27–28
registry system, of TQI (QuILTSS Institute), 114–115
Remodeling the House (Illinois ECE Story)
  adopt and implement competencies in learning journey and credentialing system step within, 108–111
  assessing competency framework fit within, 59–60
  career pathway model within, 30, 47, 108
  constituent feedback within, 60–62
  deconstruction-construction approach of, 46–47
  define the pathway problem step within, 29–32
  develop competency assessment step within, 90–99
  direct pathway within, 108
  draft competency statements step within, 57–62
  drafting representative performance indicators within, 58–59
  entitled pathway within, 108
  establish competency measurability step within, 72–78
  establish the competency framework step within, 45–49

INDEX   *143*

evaluating the impact of competencies over time and supporting competency sustainability step within, 123–124
families and communities (FCR) within, 90–91
formal standards within, 45
funding for, 110
Health, Safety, and Wellness (HSW) within, 91, 92–97, 98, 124
Human Growth and Development (HGD), 58–59, 61, 72
initial learning journey development within, 110–111
Interactions, Relationships, and Environments (IRE), 73–78
leveling within, 47, 48
Observation and Assessment competency area within, 72–73
primary content set within, 45–46
sequencing within, 46–47
settings regarding, 45
stakeholder feedback within, 109
statement vetting within, 60–62
toolboxes within, 124
See also Gateways to Opportunity ECE Credentials system
representative performance indicators, 58–59, 62. *See also* performance indicators
Road Map of Core Competencies for the Direct Service Workforce (Building From a Blueprint), 50

scoring tool
  assessment experience matching within, 89
  binary, 84
  within Building From a Blueprint (Tennessee LTSS Story), 79–82
  example of, 81
  of Health, Safety, and Wellness (HSW), 98
  of Interactions, Relationships, and Environments (IRE), 75–77
  leveled, 84–85
  performance criteria and, 72
  for performance indicators, 71
  reflection and feedback for, 85
  within Remodeling the House (Illinois ECE Story), 75–77
sequencing, 46–47, 53, 54
simulation scenario, assessment, 100–101, 103
skill, within developmental progression, 48
staff training, for incentivization, 125–126
Stakeholder Advisory Group (Building From a Blueprint), 63
stakeholders
  assessment experience review by, 89, 102–103
  establishing, 72
  organization of, 68
  performance indicator input from, 105–106
  within Remodeling the House (Illinois ECE Story), 109
students, meeting demands of, 3–5
subject matter experts (SMEs), 52
systemic competency integration, 106

teaching assistant, within early childhood education (ECE), 30
TennCare (Tennessee), Bureau of, 33–38, 63, 125–126. *See also* Building From a Blueprint (Tennessee LTSS Story)
Tennessee Career and Education Pathway website, 116
Tennessee Promise, 53
Tennessee Reconnect, 53
TQI (QuILTSS Institute)
  badges from, 110, 111, 114, 115–116
  career pathways within, 115–116
  characteristics of, 114
  coaches within, 113
  courses within, 113

credential from, 114
cue card within, 112
knowledge building within, 111–112
leveling and sequencing by, 53
origin of, 37–38
registry system of, 114–115
scaffolding within, 111–112
stakeholder needs within, 50
workforce development programs of, 49
See also Building From a Blueprint (Tennessee LTSS Story)
transparency, 3, 31, 107
tuition, charging methods for, 8–9

up-skilling, 3–4

verbs, indicator, 70, 72–73, 79, 82–83

work-based learning opportunities, within career pathways approach, 14
workforce
  challenges of, 122
  coaches/mentors within, 113–114
  pathway problems within, 28–29, 127–128
  preparing graduates for, 5–6
  questions regarding, 39
workforce development (WFD) training, 51–52, 111. *See also* Building From a Blueprint (Tennessee LTSS Story)
working backward, 80. *See also* backward design

For Product Safety Concerns and Information please contact our EU representative GPSR@taylorandfrancis.com
Taylor & Francis Verlag GmbH, Kaufingerstraße 24, 80331 München, Germany

www.ingramcontent.com/pod-product-compliance
Lightning Source LLC
Chambersburg PA
CBHW071412300426
44114CB00016B/2271